Food Culture in Central America

Food Culture in
Central America

MICHAEL R. MCDONALD

Food Culture around the World

Ken Albala, Series Editor

GREENWOOD PRESS
An Imprint of ABC-CLIO, LLC

A B C ☽ C L I O

Santa Barbara, California • Denver, Colorado • Oxford, England

Library of Congress Cataloging-in-Publication Data

McDonald, Michael R. (Michael Robert), 1961–

    Food culture in Central America / Michael R. McDonald.
      p. cm. — (Food culture around the world)
    Includes bibliographical references and index.
    ISBN 978-0-313-34767-2 (hard copy : alk. paper) — ISBN 978-0-313-34768-9
(ebook) 1. Cookery—Central America. 2. Food habits—Central America. I. Title.
    TX716.C45M34 2009
    394.1'209728—dc22   2009015629

13   12   11   10   09   1   2   3   4   5

This book is also available on the World Wide Web as an eBook.
Visit www.abc-clio.com for details.

ABC-CLIO, LLC
130 Cremona Drive, P.O. Box 1911
Santa Barbara, California 93116-1911

This book is printed on acid-free paper ∞
Manufactured in the United States of America

The publisher has done its best to make sure the instructions and/or recipes in this book are correct. However, users should apply judgment and experience when preparing recipes, especially parents and teachers working with young people. The publisher accepts no responsibility for the outcome of any recipe included in this volume.

Contents

Series Foreword

The appearance of the Food Culture around the World series marks a definitive stage in the maturation of Food Studies as a discipline to reach a wider audience of students, general readers, and foodies alike. In comprehensive interdisciplinary reference volumes, each on the food culture of a country or region for which information is most in demand, a remarkable team of experts from around the world offers a deeper understanding and appreciation of the role of food in shaping human culture for a whole new generation. I am honored to have been associated with this project as series editor.

Each volume follows a series format, with a chronology of food-related dates and narrative chapters entitled Introduction, Historical Overview, Major Foods and Ingredients, Cooking, Typical Meals, Eating Out, Special Occasions, and Diet and Health. (In special cases, these topics are covered by region.) Each also includes a glossary, bibliography, resource guide, and illustrations.

Finding or growing food has of course been the major preoccupation of our species throughout history, but how various peoples around the world learn to exploit their natural resources, come to esteem or shun specific foods, and develop unique cuisines reveals much more about what it is to be human. There is perhaps no better way to understand a culture, its values, preoccupations, and fears than by examining its attitudes toward food. Food provides the daily sustenance around which families and communities bond. It provides the material basis for rituals through which people celebrate the passage of life stages and their connection to divinity. Food preferences also serve to separate individuals and groups from each other, and as one of the most powerful factors in the construction of identity, we physically, emotionally, and spiritually become what we eat. By studying the foodways of people different from ourselves, we also grow to understand and tolerate the rich diversity of practices around the world. What seems strange or frightening among other people becomes perfectly rational when set in context. It is my hope that readers will gain from these volumes not only an aesthetic appreciation for the glories of the many culinary traditions described, but also ultimately a more profound respect for the peoples who devised them. Whether it is eating New Year's dumplings in China, folding tamales with friends in Mexico, or going out to a famous Michelin-starred restaurant in France, understanding these food traditions helps us to understand the people themselves.

As globalization proceeds apace in the 21st-century, it is also more important than ever to preserve unique local and regional traditions. In many cases these books describe ways of eating that have already begun to disappear or have been seriously transformed by modernity. To know how and why these losses occur today also enables us to decide what traditions, whether from our own heritage or that of others, we wish to keep alive. These books are thus not only about the food and culture of peoples around the world, but also about ourselves and who we hope to be.

Ken Albala
University of the Pacific

Introduction

To describe Central American food culture is a considerable task that most certainly begins with sorting out terminology. *Food culture* is a concept used throughout this book to refer to the shared beliefs, thoughts, behaviors, and practices relating to the production, distribution, preparation, and consumption of food. The book proceeds from the premise that food is more than simply a source of nutrients that allows people to survive and reproduce. Food must, of course, be produced. How, when, from where, and even why different kinds of food are produced, is a vital facet of food culture. As a cultural artifact, food also provides insight into social relations. Foods often carry important symbolic meaning and communicate about status, gender role, and even membership in the group, whether ethnic, religious, or social. Food also distinguishes for the consumer differences between the sacred and the profane, the ordinary and the special occasion. Every spoonful of soup traveling from the bowl to the mouth carries nutrients; lessons of history, geography, and politics; messages about gender, values, and morals from folklore and religion; and, not least, gustatory pleasure. Thus food culture must be studied holistically. This introduction provides a brief overview of the geography and climate of Central America, as well as a statement on the philosophy of Central American food.

Chapter 1 presents a historical overview of the region as a setting for human food culture activities beginning with prehistoric human activity following the rise and fall of complex Mesoamerican societies. Particular aspects of food culture production and consumption are recounted up to and beyond the encounter with the Old World. The chapter examines the uses of food in colonial machinations, as well as indigenous accommodations of the same.

The important foods and ingredients, techniques, and lore associated with food preparation are surveyed in Chapters 2 and 3.

Typical meals, ones taken at home with family, are the most intimate part of a food culture. These are presented in Chapter 4, with attention given to the cultural context in which those meals take place including regional or national differences.

Not all meals are taken at home, however, and Chapter 5 examines the options for Central Americans to eat a snack on the street or a meal in a modest *comedor* or fancy restaurant. Like people in all parts of the world, Central Americans mark important events or special occasions in their lives with food. They have numerous occasions to celebrate, including religious, agricultural, and official holidays. Chapter 6 examines several common festivals, including Christmas and *Semana Santa* and lifecycle rituals such as the *quinceañera*. The chapter also describes the role of foods in special occasions that involve friends, family, and the entire community.

Chapter 7 includes data and descriptive accounts of malnutrition, hunger, anemia, obesity, and other illnesses that arise in relation to poverty, diet, and food culture. The chapter also reviews current and past programs meant to ameliorate particular food-related social problems. The text concludes with a guide for resources on each of the chapter subjects and general information about the food culture of Central America.

GEOGRAPHY AND CLIMATE

Central America is a funnel-shaped, tropical isthmus, occupying an area of 230,000 square miles thrusting southeasterly to connect the North and South American continents. In geological terms, Central America is delimited to the north by the Isthmus of Tehuantepec in southern Mexico and the Isthmus of Panamá in the south. More than a mere land bridge, however, Central America is an evolutionarily complex mini-continent with great diversity in both marine and terrestrial species of plants and animals. Mountains cover nearly three-quarters of the surface area with coastal plains of varying widths on the Pacific Ocean lying to the west and southwest, and on the Caribbean Sea and the Gulf of Mexico lying to the north and east, respectively. Rainfall is abundant and perennial on the Atlantic coast, whereas the highlands and Pacific coasts have more pronounced rainy and dry seasons.

Central America is situated on a particularly unstable region of the earth's crust—the western edge of the Caribbean plate at a point of subduction and uplift. The isthmus, consequently, has at least 109 volcanoes including 11 that are currently active. Earthquakes, too, occur with some regularity in the region. In the 20th century alone, earthquakes twice destroyed Managua, the capital of Nicaragua. More recently, two significant earthquakes occurred in El Salvador in 2001; in 2003 an earthquake occurred on the border of Panamá and Costa Rica and a magnitude 6.8 tremor hit Guatemala in 2007. Volcanism has mixed blessings, however, as the fertile soils from weathered volcanic lavas have enabled abundant growth of food plants, both domesticated and wild. This has made it possible to sustain dense populations in the agriculturally productive areas from prehistoric times through the present.

Politically, Central America consists of seven independent countries. Moving from north to south, these include Belize, Guatemala, El Salvador, Honduras, Nicaragua, Costa Rica, and Panamá. With the exception of Belize, all of these countries were first settled by the Spanish in the early 1500s and remained part of the Spanish Empire until their independence. Spanish is widely spoken in the region and is the official language of all countries except Belize, who, as a former British colony, retains English as the official language for affairs of government, education, and commerce. Between one-half and two-thirds of the more than 40 million people in the region live in the urban areas of each state. During the 1960s and 1970s, Central America had one of the highest population growth rates in the world and, although it has declined since then, population growth has remained relatively high (2.1% per year in the 1990s).

Belize

The British and Spanish vied for control in many parts of the region including what is now known as Belize. Formed as an official British colony (known as British Honduras) in 1862, Belize gained its own independence in 1981. Belize—the name may come from the Mayan word for muddy water—remains a member of the British Commonwealth of Nations with Queen Elizabeth II of the United Kingdom as the titular head of state. This is arguably the most culturally complex country of the region, with roughly 40 percent of the population classified as mestizo or mixed Spanish and Maya ancestry. Another 30 percent are classified as Creoles or people of mixed African and European descent. Maya Indians account for 10 percent of the population and another 6 percent is Garifuna (people of African and American Indian descent). Belize was once dependent wholly on timber and agricultural exports, but more recently tourism has become the main-stay of the economy.

Costa Rica

Costa Rica was optimistically named the "rich coast" by Spanish explorers. Costa Rica may have been a disappointment in terms of wealth and ended up a neglected colonial backwater, home primarily to small farming communities. Today, Costa Rica stands apart in Central America. In a region often beset by turmoil and poverty, Costa Rica has become the darling of international development organizations who point out their impressive ranking on the Human Development Index (48th worldwide), which subsumes a relatively high standard of living, widespread land ownership, high rates of literacy, and low rates of infant mortality. Much credit for this achievement is given to Costa Rica's decision to abolish its military following a brief civil war in 1948. Environmentalists, too, applaud the *Ticos* (a name Costa Ricans call themselves) for their beautiful natural resources and green efforts to protect them. In 2006, Costa Rica pledged to be the first country to become carbon neutral by 2021, as evidenced by their climb up the Environmental Performance Index, from 15th place in 2006 to fifth in 2008. Although it still maintains a large agricultural sector, Costa Rica has expanded its economy to include manufacturing, technology, and tourist industries.

El Salvador

El Salvador was known at the time of the conquest as *Cuzhcatl*, or *Cuzcatlan*, which means "The Land of Precious Things" in the Nahua language. Under Spanish rule it became known as "the savior of the world" or El Salvador. It is the smallest country in Central America and is bordered by Guatemala to the west and Honduras to the north and east. It is the only Central American country without an Atlantic coastline and is situated on a fertile volcanic plateau on the Pacific coast. Known as a coffee republic for decades, El Salvador has made efforts to broaden its economic base and institute democratic reforms after a protracted civil war in the 1980s. The population is nearing 6 million people, 90 percent of whom are classified as mestizo.

Guatemala

With a name meaning "land of trees," Guatemala is heavily forested and heavily peopled, with the largest population in Central America.

Guatemala is bordered by Belize and Honduras to the east and El Salvador to the southeast. The country is very mountainous, with a small Caribbean coast and a much larger Pacific coastline. There are more than 12.7 million Guatemalans, more than half of whom are mestizos (known in Guatemala as Ladinos). Indigenous Maya people form the balance of the population. Many Maya still live in rural mountain villages, with much of their clothing and food still produced in the traditional way. Crops, such as coffee, sugar, bananas, and cacao are grown both for consumption in Guatemala and for the export market.

Honduras

Honduras, which means "the depths" in Spanish, was long inhabited by numerous indigenous peoples including the bellicose Lencas, Jicaques, and Paya hunters and fishermen before its "discovery" and naming by Christopher Columbus. Honduras is mostly mountainous, with a long and wide coastal plain. Barrier islands skirt both the Caribbean coast to the north and the smaller Pacific coast to the southwest. In the east are the swamps and forests of *La Mosquitia* or the Mosquito Coast. Owing to the diverse environments rich with plant and animal species and impressive Maya ruins, Honduras draws many international visitors but remains one of the poorest countries in the Western Hemisphere. The population is 90 percent mestizo, and the economy is based primarily on agriculture, with more than a third of the labor force involved in this sector. Major export crops include bananas, coffee, palm oil, fruit, and beef. The major subsistence crops are maize, sorghum, beans, and rice. U.S. corporate interests, especially the United Fruit Company, and a series of military dictators dominated Honduran economic life during the first half of the 20th century.

Nicaragua

The largest country in Central America, Nicaragua is named after the Nicarao, a Nahuatl-speaking tribe that inhabited the shores of Lago de Nicaragua, and the Spanish word for water, *agua*. The country is bordered by Honduras on the northwest and on the south by Costa Rica. A range of volcanic mountains divides the Caribbean lowlands and La Mosquitia from the lakes and the fertile Pacific coast where most of Nicaragua's population has always been concentrated. Mestizos make up about 77 percent of the population. Another 10 percent are of European descent, 9 percent are of African descent, and 4 percent are indigenous. Spanish is the official language, but English is spoken in the Caribbean coastal area as well.

Panamá

Panamá, an indigenous word meaning "an abundance of fish" or "abundance of butterflies," is situated on the narrow Isthmus of Panamá. It has a rugged terrain with two heavily forested mountain ranges in the eastern and western sections of the country. A third minor range extends southward along the Pacific coast into Colombia. Panamá also has more than 1,600 islands, including the San Blas Islands in the Caribbean and the Pearls Archipelago in the Gulf of Panamá. Colonized by Spain in the 1500s, Panamá gained independence in 1819, allied with Colombia initially and, with U.S. assistance, seceded in 1903. Independent Panamá promptly signed a treaty with the United States that allowed for the construction and management of the Panamá Canal. A later agreement completed transfer of the canal from the United States to Panamá in the year 2000. Agriculture is a minor part of the economy, but Panamá is self-sufficient in bananas, sugar, rice, maize and coffee production, yet imports large quantities of other foods. Bananas are the leading export product and the banana industry is an important source of rural employment. Panamá has a diverse population with a mestizo majority. About 100,000 indigenous people live in isolation in eastern Panamá and on the San Blas Islands.

THE CENTRAL AMERICAN *METATE* AND A PHILOSOPHY OF FOOD

Made of soft volcanic stone, the *metate* is a platter-size, slightly concave platform that is sometimes elevated on short legs. The *mano* is a large cylindrical stone that is rolled or rocked on the surface to grind or mix the ingredients. From prehistoric times well into the 20th century, this familiar and simple technology was used primarily to transform the coarse vegetative products of Mesoamerican agriculture into the familiar *tamales, tortillas, casabes, atoles, pepiáns,* and *moles* of Central American cuisine. With the conquest, indigenous populations from northern Mexico to Chile confronted not only the weapons and diseases of the conquistadors but a new alimentary universe that included foods such as rice, wheat and barley, citrus, onions, garlic, sugarcane, carrots, bananas, coffee, dairy foods, pork, chicken, beef, and fats.

The simple technology of *metate y mano* allowed indigenous Central Americans to make culinary sense of these novelties by combining them in some fashion with the familiar maize, beans, peppers, yuca, potatoes, and cacao of their own tradition. The development of a new Central American diet did not necessarily require wholesale replacement of the old for the new; rather, old and new were folded together to produce one of the world's first fusion cuisines. Consider for instance *chirmol frito*, a cooked tomato sauce seasoned with jalapeño peppers, garlic, limejuice, mint leaves, oregano, and parsley and often served on roasted meats or *chiles rellenos*, a globally popular stuffed-pepper dish. This sauce has as many ingredients of European and Asian provenance as those from the New World; yet no one would attribute this dish to any other part of the world.

Scholars, writers, artists, and politicians have all used the concept of *mestizaje* to capture the intense hybrid mixture of identities found in Mexico and throughout Latin America. *Mestizaje* is celebrated as a source of creativity, strength, synthesis, movement, and transformation. Much like *mestizaje*, the *metate* and *mano* provide a potent concept to capture the essence of Central American food culture. Although many *metates* have been retired and replaced by steel grinders, food processors, and other modern conveniences, this book underscores the living process of *metatezation*. Used hereafter in the text, the term refers to the grinding and melding of disparate ingredients as the means to create emergent flavors and textures. *Metatezation* is also an effective adaptation and a delicious metaphor for the change and synthesis that marks the emergence of Central American food culture and presages its future trajectory.

Timeline

c. 30,000 B.C.E.   Asian migrants cross Bering Land bridge and enter North America.

13,000–9000 B.C.E.: Paleo Indian period

Inferences of big-game hunting.

11,000–3500 B.C.E.: Archaic period

Central American people became larger, more sedentary, and more complex. Specializations in agriculture and ceramics arose during this time.

7500 B.C.E.   Early maize samples are documented at the Los Ladrones cave site in Panamá.

5000 B.C.E.   Earliest evidence of *metates* (platter-size, slightly concave platform that is sometimes elevated on short legs) and *molcajetes* (mortar and pestle) used for food processing is discovered.

4100 B.C.E.   Evidence of lime-soaking pots for maize processing is found.

4000–3500 B.C.E.   Evidence of incised and stamp-decorated pottery in Guatemala is documented.

2500 B.C.E.–300 C.E.: Preclassic or Formative period

2400 B.C.E.	Stone Maya solar calendars first appear.
2000 B.C.E.	First Olmec glyph writing is evidenced.
1000 B.C.E.	Mayan civilization emerges.
c. 50 C.E.	Maya leave first written records and first evidence of clay *comales* (flat clay cooking vessels).
First century	El Mirador, Maya city-state in northern Guatemala, is at its height of cultural expression.
250–600	In Guatemala and Honduras, consolidated city-states with substantial social class differentiation emerge; writing, sculpture, mathematics, ceramics, and large-scale urban planning are undertaken.
c. 250	Maya begin building large pyramids.

600–800: The Late Classic period

890	Maya produce first book in the Americas.
900	Great Maya cities of Central America are deserted.

900–1492: Postclassic period

1000	Reduced population cluster documented in small riverine and lakeside settlements, which are connected by trade networks.
1400	Numerous screenfold books are painted on fig-bark paper by Maya priests recording Maya mythology, theology, calendar information, and history. Of these codices, only four survive the conquest.
1493	Christopher Columbus's second voyage brings sugarcane and other Old World domesticates to Caribbean.
1502	Columbus's fourth voyage makes landfall at Honduras, Nicaragua, Costa Rica, and the Isthmus of Panamá.

1504–1823: Colonial period

1504–40	Waves of European domesticated plants and animals plus weeds, bugs, and diseases are introduced to Central America.
1510	Native population declines dramatically as a result of disease, military conflict, and brutal working conditions.

1513	Spanish explorer Vasco Núñez de Balboa sees the Pacific Ocean.
1522	Spanish expedition sets out from Panamá to settle the area to the north and names the land Costa Rica.
1523–34	Spanish conquistador Pedro de Alvarado defeats the indigenous resistance in El Salvador, Guatemala, and Honduras.
1537	Pope Paul III decides that Indians have souls and prompts development of new laws to protect them.
1563	First permanent Spanish settlement in Costa Rica, called Cartago, is established in the central highlands.
1574	Nicaraguan Bishop Gomez Fernandez de Cordoba is transferred to Guatemala and ministers to the natives until his death in 1598.
1576	Plague epidemic decimates indigenous population in Central America.
1578	Panamá becomes important commercial center and transshipment center for bullion for shipment to Spain.
1620	English baymen begin to settle in area around the Belize River to cut mahogany and log wood timbers.
1697	Itzá Maya, the last independent Maya polity located in Lake Petén Itzá, northern Guatemala, falls under Spanish rule.
1723	Eruption of the Irazú volcano destroys the town of Cartago in central Costa Rica, where a few small Spanish settlements subsist on agriculture.
1739	Panamá City becomes part of the Viceroyalty of New Granada.
1775	Powerful earthquake destroys Antigua, Guatemala. The capital city is rebuilt three years later at the present site of Guatemala City.
1790	Indigo trade reaches height of production, replacing cacao on Pacific slopes of Guatemala and El Salvador.
1798	British defeat the Spanish in Battle of St. George's Caye, Belize.

| 1823 | Guatemala, El Salvador, Honduras, Nicaragua, and Costa Rica are included in the independent Mexican Empire. |

1838–present: Republic period

1838	The Central American Confederation dissolves.
1848–60	The British establish protectorate over Mosquito Coast.
1852	U.S. entrepreneur Cornelius Vanderbilt begins passenger service across Nicaragua via steamship and carriage.
1856	U.S. soldier of fortune William Walker becomes dictator of Nicaragua for brief period.
1870s	Bananas are introduced as a cash crop to Costa Rica and soon the "miracle fruit" expands across Central America, consolidated by the Boston-based United Fruit Company in 1899. The crop becomes so critical economically that the Central American countries are dubbed "The Banana Republics."
1881–89	The French attempt to dig the Panamá Canal ends in failure.
1884	Costa Rica grants 99-year lease on 800,000 acres to Minor Keith, founder of United Fruit Company.
1903	Panamá gains independence from Colombia. United States is granted exclusive control over 10-mile wide corridor across isthmus.
1914	Panamá Canal opens, joining Pacific and Atlantic; Canal Zone is leased to the United States.
1932	Uprising by Indian workers in the coffee plantations of El Salvador ends in the death of thousands at the hands of the army and paramilitary groups.
1934	Anastasio Somoza, commander of the National Guard, organizes a coup d'etat in Nicaragua.
1945	Food and Agriculture Organization (FAO) of United Nations is founded.
1948	Costa Rica abolishes its army.
1951	Jacobo Arbnez, president of Guatemala, expropriates the land holdings of the United Fruit Company.

1964	British Honduras is granted self-government.
1968	Catholic Bishops in Central America develop the concept of Liberation Theology in response to oppressive regimes.
1969	Honduras and El Salvador fight the short-lived Football War (or Soccer War).
1972 December 23	Earthquake of 6.5 magnitude strikes Managua, Nicaragua; between 5,000 and 7,000 people are killed.
1973	The name British Honduras is changed to Belize. Global oil crisis occurs.
1974	Hurricane Fifi hits Belize, Guatemala, and Honduras; nearly 10,000 are killed.
1976 February 4	Numerous earthquakes occur near Guatemala City, Guatemala, killing 23,000, injuring 80,000, and leaving 1.5 million homeless.
1978	Hurricane Greta strikes Belize, Honduras, and Guatemala, resulting in massive damage to plantations, but causing few deaths.
1979	Opponents of the Sandinista government flee Nicaragua for Honduras, where they become known as Contra Rebels.

1980s–1990s: The Lost Decade

1986	In the Iran-Contra Affair, the United States secretly sells arms to Iran and channels the proceeds to the Contra rebels.
October 10	Earthquake with a magnitude of 7.5 hits San Salvador, El Salvador. The death toll is about 1,500, with 20,000 people injured and more than 300,000 homeless.
1987	Costa Rican President Oscar Arias Sanchez is awarded the Nobel Peace Prize.
1989	United States launches Operation Just Cause, a military invasion of Panamá, ousting General Manuel Antonio Noriega.

1992	Earthquake of 7.0 magnitude strikes the Pacific coast of Nicaragua and kills 120 people; more than 16,000 are left homeless.

1997 An accord is signed by Guatemala, Belize, Honduras, and Mexico to protect their shared Caribbean coral reef system.

1998 Hurricane Mitch hits Honduras, Nicaragua, Guatemala, and Belize, causing massive damage to agriculture and infrastructure. The death toll is over 18,000.

2001
January and February Two earthquakes leave a wake of destruction in north and central El Salvador, killing more than 1,000 people and affecting nearly a quarter of its 6.2 million population. Poor rural communities, which spend 70 percent of their income on food, are the worst-hit.

A month-long drought ravages Central America with crop losses nearing 80 percent in Honduras, Guatemala, parts of El Salvador, and Nicaragua.

2003
December 25 Strong earthquake shakes the border of Costa Rica and Panamá.

2005 Central American Free Trade Agreement with United States is signed into effect by Guatemala, Honduras, El Salvador, Nicaragua, Costa Rica, and the Dominican Republic.

September 5 Hurricane Stan knocks down trees, washes out bridges, causes mud slides, and kills 65 people in the region.

2006 Daniel Ortega wins the Nicaraguan presidential election, returning to power after a 16-year absence.

July 11 Central American presidents agree to ease border controls and install a common customs system modeled after the EU. Agreement would allow residents to cross borders without passports or visas.

New environmental report identifies fertilizer runoff from commercial agricultural plantations in Belize, Guatemala, and Honduras as a threat to the Caribbean coral reef system and tourism.

2007

June 13   A magnitude 6.8 earthquake hits Guatemala.

September 6   Category 5 Hurricane Felix hits Nicaragua and kills 40
                            people.

November 5   Jurors in America rule that American companies Dole
                            and Dow are responsible for injuries and illnesses suf-
                            fered by banana workers in Nicaragua during the 1970s
                            and 1980s.

2008   Central American leaders at the World Economic Forum
                            on Latin America warn that the impact of climbing food
                            and oil prices could undo recent gains made by econo-
                            mies.

2009

January 8   An earthquake in North Central Costa Rica kills 34
                            people.

2012

December 22   Maya calendar ends. According to the Mayan prophecy,
                            the world will be forever altered by a series of powerful
                            earthquakes.

1

Historical Overview

In Central America, food is inseparable from its lengthy and complex history. Blessed with natural riches and diverse biota, Central America includes thousands of marine and terrestrial species of plants and animals, rich volcanic soils, and moderate climates. These resources provide the region with the raw materials necessary to become one of the great hearths of civilization. New World agriculture began in Central America. People domesticated plants and some animals and, by refining their qualities through careful selection and preservation, were able to meet the food needs of populations numbering in the millions. This accomplishment, along with scores of other agricultural and culinary innovations, marks the dawn of Central American food culture. Although the history begins long before the isthmus was discovered, the arrival of Europeans provided an important and essential centripetal force to bring together the plants, animals, and people necessary for the full flavor of Central America to emerge.

INDIGENOUS AMERICANS

Two important sources of information contribute to the understanding of the food culture of native Central Americans before the time of the conquest. The first is the abundance of archaeological information: settlement sites, monumental architecture, and even skeletal remains that reveal, among other things, the what, how, and where people ate. Other insights are gained from written accounts of the same activities. Among the conquistadors were astute observers and chroniclers who provided in their diaries and reports to Rome and Madrid detailed aspects of food production, preparation, preservation, allocation, and even disposal at the time of first contact. Particularly in the case of the Maya, historic written accounts translated from the Maya glyphs, books, and other records survived the conquest to lend further insiders' views on important aspects of food culture.

Archaeological Accounts

With slightly different boundaries and purpose in mind, archaeologists delimit *Mesoamerica* as a culture area lying partially within Central America. Mesoamerica subsumes a number of pre-Columbian societies that flourished in an area extending from central Honduras and northwestern Costa Rica on the south to south-central Mexico on the north. The Mesoamerican culture area includes only the stratified agrarian pre-Columbian civilizations including the Olmec, the Maya, and the Aztec. As a category, Mesoamerican societies shared high levels of technological skill, monumental construction, similar myths of origin, complex calendars and writing systems, and, most important, intensive, large-scale production of the dietary staples: maize, beans, and squash.

Not all indigenous peoples in Central America attained the same degree of cultural complexity. Those living in the lowlands and coastal plains settled down in agrarian communities somewhat later and used less-intensive, shifting techniques of food production. People there grew root crops including cassava and yams in small mixed plots that would be abandoned after a brief time in production. As gardens were moved periodically, entire villages would follow, leaving less permanent footprints on the landscape and therefore less evidence for later scholars to contemplate. Bands of foragers and horticultural chiefdoms lived in the periphery of Mesoamerica. They were found along both coasts all the way to the Isthmus of Panamá in what is known in the archaeological literature as the Intermediate area.[1] This area was once dismissed as inferior to Mesoamerica, but recent archaeological work indicates that it was home to some of the earliest cultivation, pottery, and metallurgy in the hemisphere. Scholars posit that it is likely that people in the Intermediate area greatly facilitated the transmission and diffusion of culture flowing both to the north and south.

The culture area concept includes both geographic and temporal boundaries, and archaeologists divide Mesoamerica into discrete time periods, defined primarily by the prevailing food-getting activity. The Mesoamerican Paleo-Indian period, for instance, occurred in the years 13,000–9500 B.C.E. and precedes the advent of agriculture. Food was acquired in this time through nomadic hunting and gathering practices. Stone spear points found in association with skeletal remains of megafauna suggest that early Mesoamericans hunted large game.

By the beginning of the Archaic period 11,000 years ago, culture was becoming more complex. People were using specialized tools and ceremonial objects, and the great variety of bones found in the remains of campfires and trash piles suggest they hunted a wide variety of game to meet their dietary needs. Geological and archaeological evidence suggests that the climate in Central America had become warmer and drier during this time, and the big game animals had become less abundant. Hunting activities were broadened to include small game including deer, rabbits, turtles, and birds. People also began to include more plant-based resources in their diet. Archaeological sites reveal that various seeds, roots, and gourds were incorporated into the diet of people living during the Archaic period in Central America.

Life in the Archaic period also involved the initial cultivation of wild plants. The Archaic was a period of transition spanning 5,000 years. It took the former gatherers of wild plants many generations to acquire the botanical knowledge needed to begin the process of domestication. Certainly, they had favorite plants and knew their growing habitats, but learning how to plant and cultivate them would have been a slow process fraught with setbacks. Eventually plants with desired qualities such as size, taste, and preservation properties came to dominate discrete areas of the landscape. By 5000 B.C.E., people were living in settlements adjacent to fields of domesticated plants. By favoring certain plants over others, Mesoamerican farmers inadvertently entered into a co-evolutionary dependency with plants like maize and beans, which are now as fully dependent on humans as humans are on them.

Domestic growth and culture change followed the Archaic period and forms of Preclassic period culture were expressed from 4000 B.C.E. to roughly 200 C.E. During this period, a further refinement of agricultural techniques led to increases in production that brought larger populations into permanent settlements, with thousands of denizens organized into increasingly complex social and occupational divisions. Mesoamericans began to build temples and pyramids in settlements that ultimately became the religious and political centers including the Maya rainforest centers of Tikal, Palenque, and Copan. The Classic period, which occurred between 200 and 900 C.E., saw further development of great urban centers. Rather than an empire proper, Maya civilization was a series of independent city-states, some with populations nearing 200,000 inhabitants. The Maya developed glyphic writing and a system for measuring time to organize agricultural work and to schedule markets, holidays, and rituals.

Calendars and Ritual

The Maya had a complex view of time and developed several interrelated systems for tracking the passage of time, including two types of calendars, one on a 260-day cycle and the other on a 365-day cycle, which approximated the solar year. This latter instrument divided the year into four seasons, marking also the two solstices and the two equinoxes that represented the four "directional pillars" that support the year. These four times of the year are still marked as important cosmic events for contemporary Maya people and as indicators of seasonal change. The solar year was divided further into 18 months consisting of 20 days, with names given to the days and months coming from animals, flowers, heavenly bodies, and other concepts with symbolic significance. The second calendar counted a year of 260 days containing one cycle of 20 day names and a second cycle of 13 numbers. Each day was known by a particular combination of number and day name. Cogged wheels representing the 20 day cycle and 13 number cycles were interconnected on a calendar device whereon the same combination of number and day name would only occur every 260 days. The two calendars were run simultaneously and each day would be named after its position in both calendars, resulting in nearly 19,000 discrete combinations and requiring a period of 52 years to complete the entire cycle.

Modern versions of the Maya calendar are still used throughout Central America today. More accurate in many ways than the contemporaneous European calendar, the Maya calendar was still less than perfect; the year was left with five uncategorized days that were considered by the Maya to be very unlucky. Every fourth year this final period was adjusted to six days to compensate for the leap year.

Each month was further associated with an agricultural activity, a particular deity, and ceremonies during which sacrificial meals were often organized to honor the particular god. As sufficient rainfall was very important for growing and harvesting the month, marking the beginning of the rainy season (roughly May) was celebrated with rituals for *Chaac*, the rain deity. Among the various *Chaac* ceremonies was one in which young boys croaked like frogs, as frogs and toads were believed to be the earthly messengers of *Chaac* who announced imminent rainfall. Other rain rituals involved sacrifices of young men and women who were thrown into cenotes (sink holes) and left to drown and enter the realm of the rain deities.

For reasons still unknown and much debated, the Classic Maya civilization collapsed in approximately 900 C.E. Many archaeologists point to the estimates of size and density of the population in the Maya region, nearing 400 people per square mile, as a prime cause of the collapse; others argue for climactic causes. Studies of human bones and teeth from burial mounds dated to this time reveal evidence of malnutrition, various communicable diseases, and great disparity between elites and the common people in terms of skeletal health. A breakdown of trade between centers likely contributed to the collapse as well.

The phase that followed the abandonment of the rainforest centers is known as the Post Classic period, which lasted from 900 C.E. to the arrival of the Spaniards in the early 1500s. Much less is known about the Post Classic period because of the comparative lack of art, artifacts, and structures. Intensive farming methods did give way to less productive forms and, expectedly, the population dropped precipitously. Still, the Maya continued to exist, albeit as numerous, often fractious polities when they encountered the Europeans on their arrival in the 16th century. For instance, archaeological data support historic accounts of a Maya principality ruled from a city called Chetumal located near the present day site of Corozal Town, Belize. A network of trade connected Chetumal with the Bay Islands of present-day Republic of Honduras. Canoes loaded with salt, slaves, fish, and cloth made the journey south from Chetumal to Ulna and returned with cacao, an important commodity that was also used as money among the Maya.

Firsthand Accounts

Life in the Post Classic Maya civilization is known further from the 16th-century diaries, letters, and other written accounts of priests and other colonialists. Among the noteworthy scribes of that time is Diego de Landa, the fourth Bishop of Yucatán. As a missionary priest, de Landa sought to learn as much of the native culture as he could, traveling by foot across the Yucatan peninsula to visit and learn about the people in the region. Upon his return to Spain in 1566, he wrote the *Relación de las Cosas de Yucatán*, which provided incredibly detailed observations and explanations of Mayan language, glyphic writing system, religion, and food culture.

Excerpt from de Landa's Relacion

Their principal diet is maize, from which they make various kinds of food and drink . . . The Indian women leave the maize to soak overnight in lime water so that in the morning it is soft and therefore partly prepared; in this fashion the husk and the stalk are separated from the grain. They grind it between stones, and while half ground, make large balls and loads of it . . . From the most finely ground maize they extract a milk which they thicken over the fire to make into a kind of porridge, which they drink hot in the morning. They throw water on what is leftover from the morning and drink it during the day because they are not accustomed to drink water on its own. . . . They extract form cacao, a grease which resembles butter, and from this and from the maize they make another drink which is both tasty and highly regarded . . . They make bread in a number of ways; and it is a good and healthy bread; but it is bad to eat cold so the Indian women go to pains to make it twice a day . . . They make stews of vegetables and the meat of deer and of wild and tame fowl, all of which may be found in large numbers. They also have good provisions, because they now breed the pigs and poultry of Castile. In the morning they drink the hot drink with peppers, which has been described, at the midday the other cold ones, and at night the stews; and if there is no meat, they make their sauces out of pepper and vegetables. The men were not accustomed to eat with the women; they ate on the floor or, at most, off a mat for a table. They eat well when they have food but when they do not they do not they endure hunger very well and survive on very little. They wash their hands and mouths after eating.[2]

No relativist or apologist, de Landa believed that the materials and behaviors he saw among the Maya were clear evidence of idolatry and devil worship. The zealous de Landa conducted his own New World version of the Inquisition where, in addition to 5,000 "idols," he burned 27 painted books or codices of Mayan writing. Only four of those original Mayan texts (codices) survived into the present era. Fortunately, some literate members of the highland Maya nobility translated pre-Columbian books into Latin script to preserve what they could of their history and cultural heritage. The most famous example of transcription is the *Popol Vuh*, the Maya creation myth. The highland Maya of Guatemala were particularly successful in preserving ancient books in this way. Two hundred years after the conquest, many ancient books, including the transcribed text of the *Popol Vuh*, were discovered cached away in secret so that Christian authorities would not learn of them.

De Landa's Inquisition included acts of torture and physical abuse on the Maya that many viewed as excessive, earning de Landa an unenviable place on the list of villains in the meta-narrative known as "la Leyenda

Negra" or the "Black Legend of Spanish Cruelty." Although based on fact, much of the legend was hyperbolic, anti-Catholic and anti-Spanish propaganda promulgated throughout Protestant Europe as part of colonial rivalries. The indictment leveled at the conquistadors resonates into the present era as prejudice against people of Spanish descent.

Precontact Indigenous Foodways

At the time of contact, Mesoamericans were producing and eating a varied and sufficient diet, but it was subject to periodic shortages brought on by warfare, drought, pestilence, or volcanic eruptions. For instance, in his accounts, de Landa records a period of hunger after a hurricane. It is likely that the majority of people worked as farmers and followed a schedule of planting, burning, harvesting, and feasting determined by the lunar calendars. The basic unit of production was the *milpa*, or garden plot, that was carved out of forested lands with the help of stone tools and fire. As farming for the Maya was both an economic and a religious undertaking, an offering by the farmer to the gods of candles and copal incense was obligatory. Then, underbrush and small trees were removed, left to dry, and burned before the summer rains. Rainwater would leach ashes into the soil and temporarily fertilize the area under cultivation. Central American farmers still practice techniques such as this to help preserve soil viability. When ready for planting, more propitiation, including sacrifices or food offerings, would be made to ask permission and blessings for planting. Using a sharpened wooden digging stick, the farmer would plant seeds of maize, beans, and squash in the same shallow holes.

The genius of this system is revealed in the complementarities of the triad. The maize sprouts first, shooting up a stalk that provides a substructure on which beans are able to climb. The beans sprout second and, as leguminous plants, are able to transfer atmospheric nitrogen underground where other plants may access the nutrient. The squash plant sprouts last and spreads horizontally along the surface of the *milpa* ground to block out space, light, and nutrients from weeds that would compete with the food plants. The creeping vines also act like a mulch to preserve moisture and retard soil erosion in the *milpa*. Other crops grown in the *milpa* were root crops such as sweet potatoes and yuca (manioc), chiles, herbs, and vegetables. The Maya also kept orchards of fruit-bearing shrubs and trees. Today the ruins of their settlements can be spotted by the groves of *ramón*, *zapotes*, *mameys*, that have surrounded the sites for a thousand years or more.

Among the tree crops, avocado was and is an important source of fat in the Maya diet. When avocado is chopped, mixed with chiles and salt, and other ingredients into a coarse paste, it becomes *guacamol,* a dish still enjoyed today.

Guacamol

3 ripe avocados, peeled, seeded, and chopped

1–2 cloves garlic, minced

1 tsp. finely minced dried Mexican oregano

juice of 1 lime

1 Tbs. olive oil

salt to taste

Place all the ingredients in a large bowl and mash with the back of a fork until pureed but still chunky.

Serve as a condiment with entrees, grilled meats, or as a dip with tortilla chips.

Domesticated Animals

There were few animals suitable for domestication in Central America, and consequently only special people such as priests and nobles regularly consumed meat food. Maya chiefs were also permitted to eat human flesh, which they did for ritual purposes such as commemorating a military victory. Everyone else ate flesh (animal) only on special occasions. Archaeological evidence indicates that turkey and ducks were domesticated approximately 5,500 years ago, but, given the abundance of the charred bones found in archaeological sites, dogs were probably the preferred source of animal protein in ancient Mesoamerica.

The Maya domesticated stingless bees and harvested their honey to sweeten some corn beverages and chocolate. Honey was used in the preparation of various alcoholic beverages including *balche,* a Maya version of mead. *Balche* was made in a trough or a canoe that was filled with water and honey and the roots and bark from the *balche* tree that ferments in short order. Celebrants believed consumption of *balche* would convey powers of divination. A state of drunkenness facilitated direct communication with supernatural forces and would enable a person to foretell the future or provide explanation for events not otherwise understood.

People also hunted wild animals such as iguana, paca, deer, rabbit, birds, and various types of insects. In the coastal areas, fish were also a major source of food and, along with salt, important commodities for trading with inland communities.

NATIVE PEOPLES

The actual number of aboriginal inhabitants of Central America at the time of European contact is unknown, but estimates range upward of 6 million.[3] Warfare, privation, slavery, and European diseases are collectively credited with reducing the native population by more than 90 percent within a few decades of contact. The native people in the region today are essentially survivors of the conquest. Somewhere between 4 and 6 million indigenous people now live in Central America, but they are by no account a homogenous group. There are more than 40 distinct indigenous populations, some with decidedly Mesoamerican characteristics, especially seed-based agriculture. Others, with their root crop-based cultures, resemble more the Indians of South America and the Caribbean. The proportion of native people varies from a tiny 1 percent in El Salvador to nearly half the population in Guatemala.

Indigenous people have struggled everywhere with and against the forces of assimilation during the last 500 years. Before the Spanish conquest in the early 1520s, three principal tribes, each with a different culture and language, inhabited Nicaragua: the Niquirano, the Chorotegano, and the Chontal. Each of these diverse groups occupied much of Nicaragua's territory in independent chiefdoms. The invading Spaniards and the epidemics that followed nearly eradicated them all. Much reduced by war and disease, the surviving indigenous people were forced to learn Spanish, adopt Catholicism, and work under slavelike conditions for the Spanish colonizers and missionary priests. During the ensuing centuries assimilation meant the gradual abandonment of Indian language and customs. The process was periodically hastened by campaigns of political repression such as the one that occurred in El Salvador after a failed uprising in 1932.

In Panamá, vestiges of the once dominant indigenous population maintain greater autonomy and distinctiveness only by living on reserves or *comarcas*. In these semiautonomous political districts, indigenous people, including the Emberá and the Kuna, maintain a traditional way of life based on fishing, hunting, and farming. They also make handicrafts and seek work in the cities, but they continue to struggle for their rights and battle discrimination in the broader society.

In other areas, indigenous groups have survived through isolation from the dominant mestizo culture in *de facto* reservations. The sparsely populated and inhospitable Caribbean lowlands of Nicaragua and Honduras for instance (the setting for Paul Theroux's 1981 novel, *The Mosquito Coast*), are home to the Miskito Indians. Before contact with Africans

and Europeans, the Miskito did not exist as a unified people.[4] Their ancestors lived in loose networks of foraging and horticultural bands numbering
fewer than 2,000, living along the coastal river basins. Their experience
with the conquest came through contact with English traders and pirates
who regularly visited the coast. Apocryphal accounts assert that the name
"Miskito" derives from "muskets," which were supplied to them by these
visitors. Weapons and isolation allowed the Miskito to subdue the neighboring indigenous groups inhabiting the Caribbean coast (Sumu and
Rama) and to develop an essentially independent and expanding kingdom throughout the colonial era.

Adding to a population and culture that grew to dominate the region
at an incredible rate in the 18th century, the Miskito assimilated runaway
African slaves and abducted other people from raids on neighboring tribes.
Like the neighboring Garifuna, the Miskito emerged in the circumstantial
confluence of mercantilism, slavery, colonialism, and piracy. They have
become the largest indigenous group in Nicaragua and the second most
widely distributed indigenous people in Central America after the Maya.[5]
With growth, settlements became more permanent and traditional subsistence practices of marine and terrestrial foraging were complemented by
an agricultural economy that incorporated new plants and animals such
as pigs, chickens, and rice. The Miskito are known more recently for their
role in the controversies surrounding turtle hunting and depletion, lobster
diving, and participation in the Nicaragua Contra War.

Finally, castelike social divisions rather than geographic or political
boundaries separate some indigenous groups from the mestizo population in other areas of Central America. An estimated 1.5 million to 4.5
million Mayan speakers, descendants of the former Maya civilization, are
the largest native group in the region. The Maya are subdivided into 20
linguistically discrete areas of Guatemala, El Salvador, Belize, and Honduras.[6] In Guatemala, some indigenous communities still adhere to their
traditional language, dress, religious practices, and diet. When the military began systematic repression of indigenous people in the mid-1970s,
many abandoned these outwardly visible ethnic markers, leaving them
largely indistinguishable from the surrounding ladino population, but safer
from persecution. Other lesser-known native groups of Central America
include the Bokotá, Boruca, Cabecar, Chorti, Guaymí, Jicaque, Lenca,
Matagalpa, Monimbo, Pech, Pipil, Sumo, Teribe, and Wounaan. Many
of these natives no longer speak their aboriginal language and have been
assimilated in other significant ways to the dominant mestizo culture. Native peoples are typically the poorest in the region, often lacking access to
basic services such as education, healthcare, and housing, as well as other
means to social mobility.

Contributions of Indigenous Foodways

According to the accounts of Diego de Landa, the precontact Maya diet was based on three meals, two of which were beverages made from *nixta-malized* maize dough. The third, the evening meal, was a soup or stew accompanied by tamale or tortilla.[7] The most significant contribution from indigenous people to the Central American diet is maize. Throughout most of the region, it is clearly the most important foodstuff and the main source of calories in the total diet. Maize is consumed fresh-roasted, in soups and stews, or fermented for beverages, and on special occasions in the form of cooked tamales. The tortilla, however, is the quintessential maize-based food. Tortillas are an all-purpose food consumed for breakfast, lunch, and diner and throughout the day as snacks across the region. Beans, of course, are another native contribution to the typical Central American meal and are a regular food item for breakfast and dinner. Indigenous people contributed many other foods to broader Central American food culture including tomatoes, avocados, squashes, and chile peppers, all of which are regularly featured in Central American meals.

EUROPEANS

On his fourth voyage in 1502, Christopher Columbus sailed to Central America, arriving at Guanaja (Isla de Pinos) in the Bay Islands off the coast of Honduras. He later landed on the American mainland at Puerto Castilla, near Trujillo, Honduras, and spent two months exploring the coasts of Honduras, Nicaragua, and Costa Rica before arriving in Almirante Bay, Panamá. On his return trip to Europe, Columbus's fleet was destroyed in a storm and he was stranded on Jamaica for nearly a year. This setback essentially ended Columbus's involvement in New World exploration, although his name, *Cristibol Colon*, continued to live on, as explorers and settlers for generations after him were known as "colonists."

Spanish initiatives continued despite Columbus' absence, and during the early 1500s, they used the major Caribbean islands of Hispaniola, Cuba, and Puerto Rico as bases for expeditions to the mainland of Central America. On one of these campaigns, the charismatic Vasco Núñez de Balboa founded the Darien colony in 1510, Spain's first truly productive colony on *Tierra Firma* (mainland America). Pedrarias Dávila, who both succeeded and executed Balboa, extended the colony, founding Panamá City in 1519 from which he launched forays of subjugation into Nicaragua and Honduras. Explorers from all parts of the empire converged and competed to conquer territory and assert Spanish control of much of Central America.

Colonial Central America was eventually divided into two jurisdictions. The territory that includes present-day Panamá was attached to New Granada (modern Colombia) in the Viceroyalty of Peru. The area from Costa Rica northward through Chiapas, a state in present-day Mexico, was known as the Kingdom of Guatemala. Although officially part of the Viceroyalty of New Spain, Guatemala was relatively autonomous with its own capital city in Antigua, which was moved later to Guatemala City, bustling with bureaucrats, clerics, and the landholding and commercial elite of the colony.

The Columbian Exchange

One of the more profound effects of the conquest has been the Columbian exchange. The concept originated in a book written in 1972 by the social historian Alfred W. Crosby that succinctly describes the interchange of fauna, and flora, in the encounters between New and Old World inhabitants as a result of Columbus's voyages.[8] For their part of the exchange, the Spanish moved horses, mules, donkeys, cattle, pigs, sheep, and goats from the Old World to Central America where they affected entire ecosystems, traditional patterns of land use, and various economic activities including transportation. Animal husbandry led to the development of social institutions such as the hacienda and occupations such as vaqueros, drovers and herders that quickly became part of the Central American economy. The introduction of beef cattle also affected the diet, bringing many meat recipes to the region including *carne en palito* meat on a stick, a favorite snack food sold from street vendor carts throughout Panamá.

Carne en Palito

1 lb. sirloin beef steak

2 Tbs. orange juice

1 Tbs. olive oil

2 Tbs. red wine

6–8 garlic cloves, crushed

2 tsp. *achiote* powder

1 tsp. ground cumin

salt and pepper to taste

Place sirloin in freezer for 1–2 hours (this makes it easier to slice). Mix the orange juice, olive oil, wine, garlic, *achiote*, cumin, salt, and pepper together to make a marinade.

Slice thin strips across the grain of the meat and skewer onto sticks.

Marinate meat in refrigerator for two or more hours. Grill on each side until done.

Plants, too, traveled across the Atlantic to the Americas, including rice, coffee, citrus, bananas, sugarcane, olives, and various fruits and herbs. Two important domesticates among those brought to the New World were wheat and grapes. Beyond the European preference for wheat bread, the grain also held religious significance. Since the beginning of Christianity, wheat bread alone has been permitted for use in the Sacrament of Transubstantiation. Grapes, too, are significant in this regard, as wine made from them is transformed into the blood of Jesus in the same ritual. As a crop, grapes were poorly suited for production in most of Central America and, although wheat flour grew in some areas, both commodities remained expensive imports from Spain. Bread and wine were symbolically and economically associated with the church and state, the most powerful institutions in the colonial social order, a fact that may have amplified their allure in the colonies.

With the exception of information gleaned from descriptive accounts of life in Guatemala or the census information gained toward the end of the colonial period, Spanish settler life is not well known.[9] Spanish society in Central America likely mirrored life in Spain with some accommodation for local conditions. Under the pretext that others might harm the indigenous peoples, Spain reserved immigration to Central America for its own citizens well into the 19th century. Except for the traffic in African slaves, foreign trade was also forbidden in Central America unless the goods passed first through Spain.

During a 300-year cultural and economic monopoly, Spanish immigrants effected massive change in the region. Most apparent are such attributes as language, religion, and the racially based, hierarchical social organization that assigned *Peninsulares* (European-born Spaniards) the top berth in the caste system. Food was one of the mechanisms used by high-status colonists to mark their identity as members of the elite. A food hierarchy emerged to parallel the social one, with foods of European provenance receiving higher esteem than those of the New World. The deliberately European manners and symbol-laden menus of Spaniards of the higher classes distinguished them from the lower orders including the American-born Spaniards known as *Criollos*. So conscious were *Peninsulares* of class distinctions, that they were known to have sent their pregnant wives back to Spain to protect their children from the reduced social status ascribed to those of American birth.

MESTIZOS

Immigrants to Central America from the peninsula were overwhelmingly male, and many colonists fathered children with Indian women through marriage, concubinage, or more ephemeral relationships. The resulting mixed-race individuals were assigned to *castas* or castes that classified them according to the extent and content of their racial mix. The categories and terminology of the caste system grew more complex over time, but the most common category was that of "mestizo," indicating someone of mixed Spanish and indigenous heritage. The term *mestizo* also designates a middling stratum distinct from and inferior to Europeans (Spaniard) but superior to Amerindians living in the region and, as such, had pejorative overtones. The Spanish notions of purity or nobility meant that "whiteness" carried social and economic advantages. Dilution, or loss of purity via mixing, was undesirable and some mixed race individuals and families affected behaviors of the higher class by wearing shoes rather than sandals and eating wheat bread rather than maize tortillas.

The mestizos or ladino (as they are known in Guatemala) cultures arose typically in the frontier settings where contact between colonists and indigenous people was most intense and exchange and modification of cultural practices most pronounced and most interesting. More a category than a distinct and homogenous ethnic group, mestizos now dominate the population of Central America, accounting for a third of the population in Belize, half in Guatemala, nearly three quarters in Nicaragua and Panamá, and 90 percent or more in Honduras and El Salvador. The exception, and perhaps only a semantic one, is Costa Rica, where 95 percent of the population is categorized as white, effectively subsuming any mestizo identity.[10] Some mestizo cultural features such as participation in the market economy, social aspirations, and tastes are clearly oriented toward European and North American ideals, whereas others including communal religious practices and kinship ties have clear, if unacknowledged, indigenous origins. Consistent with their name, mestizo often mix traditional indigenous dishes, mainly preparations of Maya origin, with old Spanish prototypes creating truly synthetic forms, fusing elements from each source.

Dulce de Güisquilles

5 güisquilles

1/2 cup sugar

2 Tbs. butter

1/2 tsp. ground cinnamon

1 tsp. vanilla

1 egg lightly beaten

2/3 cup finely crushed (with a rolling pin) *champurradas* or sugar cookies

1/3 cup raisins

1/3 cup sliced white almonds

Wash and peel the *güisquilles*. Cut into quarters and remove centers. Cut again into halves and place in large pot with enough water to cover. Cook until tender, about 20 minutes. Set aside to cool. Puree *güisquilles* in food processor or blender. In medium saucepan, melt butter on low heat, add puree and egg, stirring until well mixed. Increase heat to medium and add crushed cookies, vanilla, cinnamon, and sugar. Stir five minutes more. Reduce heat and mix in raisins and almonds. Remove from heat. Serve warm in small dessert bowls.[11]

ANTILLEAN OR AFRO-LATIN AMERICANS

Stretching along the Caribbean coast are populations of black or mixed race, English-speaking and Protestant people, primarily of West Indian (Antillean) heritage. They presently constitute approximately 4 percent of the population across the region, with higher concentrations found in Belize and Panamá, as these two Central American states participated in the colonial slave economy to a greater degree than did their neighbors. As was the practice in the British West Indies, African slaves were brought to Belize to work in the mahogany industry in such great numbers that, by the middle of the 18th century, Africans and their descendents constituted the majority group in the population of the colony. Years of interaction and intermarriage with many other ethnic groups resulted in a mixed ethnic group known as Creole or "Kriol" who are descended wholly or in part from African slaves. The term is similar to the Spanish colonial category of *Criollo*, in as much as they both share the attribute of American birth and some notion of mixing. The term *Creole*, *Kreyol*, or *Kweyol* also has meaning with respect to languages spoken the by people of the same name. Creole languages are also derived from a fusion of elements: African and European lexicons and syntax are joined to make the lingua franca of Belize. Somewhere between 24 and 40 percent of the population of Belize now define themselves as Creole and speak the local creolized English dialect known as Kriol.

   A similar history of slavery dating back to the 16th century in Panamá accounts for part of the black population found there today. Although the number of slaves was small compared to insular Caribbean plantations, the descendents of maroons and freed blacks play important roles in society and in defining Panamanian culture. The native black population came to be referred to as *negros coloniales* or *nativos* in distinction from the *negros antillanos* who came in the tens of thousands from the British West Indies during the early part of the 20th century to work on the canal, railroads, and banana plantations. A transient mindset, language, and cultural norms initially separated the Antillean migrants from the Spanish-speaking populace. The West Indians' association with North Americans in the Canal Zone and plantations led to further friction with "latinized" Panamanian blacks.

   Other English-speaking cultural enclaves of Antillean transplants arose in places throughout Central America including the Limón Province of Costa Rica. Slavery brought the first wave of blacks to Costa Rica and more migrated, along with other ethnic groups, to become workers on Costa Rican railroads and fruit plantations in the late 1800s. As noncitizens, the black migrant workers were segregated and most of the country was off limits to them. The apartheid-like laws were abolished in 1948, but their effect was to concentrate Caribbean migrants into outlier communities in Limón province where an Antillean orientation and identity was maintained. English language and West Indian customs are still common, but the Caribbean links and distinctions have abated somewhat. The older Afro-Caribbean identified population is dying out, and the younger generation is intermarrying, speaking Spanish, and generally opting for inclusion into Costa Rican society.

   Elsewhere geography served to enforce segregation much as it had for indigenous Central Americans; most Creoles reside in communities near the Caribbean coasts. About 9 percent of the population of Nicaragua is black and, as elsewhere, trace their descent from the former slaves and indentured laborers brought to the region when it was a British protectorate. In Honduras and Guatemala, roughly 2 percent of the population is black and many speak creolized English. The lack of a Caribbean coast and thereby access to the slave trade explains in part why El Salvador is the only Central American country without a significant black population. More explanation is found in the longstanding immigration laws prohibiting blacks from entering the country until their repeal in the 1980s. The few Salvadorans with African heritage are most likely located in San Salvador, the capital, and the port city of La Union.

Antillean immigrants have contributed derived African elements and manners of preparation to extend the range of the typical meal in Central America. New tastes and agricultural products, including ackee, okra, breadfruit, and coconut, became important foodstuffs for many Afro-Antillean recipes. A particular example of Afro-Antillean influence on Central American food culture is *fufu*, a term of African origin used to describe any boiled, mashed starch such as plantains or yams. Other ingredients are added to the mash such as fried onions, garlic, olive oil, and vinegar, along with seasoned morsels of chicken or bacon. Found from Belize to the Bocas del Toros islands of Panamá, *fufu*-based meals are especially popular. The term is sometimes also used in reference to an entire stew composed of a coconut milk base, boiled and mashed plantains, chilies, yuca, yams, and fried fish.

Souse or *saos* is another African-influenced dish diffused from Jamaican foodways that consists of boiled calf's or pig's feet plus other parts such as snouts and ears marinated in limejuice, onions, chiles, salt, and pepper. Following the same migratory path from the insular eastern Caribbean, other dishes have become part of creole Central American cuisine including johnnycakes, dried codfish, and ginger beer.

Saos (Souse)

3–4 large fresh pork hocks plus other parts if available (ears, snouts)

2 cups cider or red wine vinegar

1 Tbs. salt

1 tsp. black pepper

1 tsp. sugar

1 Tbs. allspice berries

4 large limes, juiced

1 large white onion, peeled and sliced

2–3 cloves garlic, chopped

2–3 Scotch bonnet or *habanero* peppers (chop and remove seeds and membranes)

3 medium cucumbers, peeled and cut into bite-size morsels

Combine vinegar, black pepper, sugar, garlic, and allspice in mixing bowl with the pork parts (hocks). If needed, add water to the bowl to cover the pork with liquid. Let stand for 20–30 minutes.

Turn the hocks over; let stand for another 20–30 minutes.

Remove the hocks from the bowl, discard the liquid, place pork parts in a soup pot with salt and water, and bring to a boil.

Turn down heat and let simmer for one hour. Rinse the pork parts under cold tap water, and allow them to cool for a few minutes. Shred/slice the meat into strips about a quarter-inch thick; discard any bones. Combine the meat in mixing bowl with the peppers, onions, cucumbers, and limejuice. Stir, cover, put in refrigerator to chill for an hour or more. Stir, serve, and enjoy.

Garifuna

The discussion of Afro-Latin American people must certainly include the Garífuna or Garinagua. Formerly known as the Black Carib, the Garifuna are a highly distinctive Central American people with a remarkable New World genesis. They trace their ancestry equally to shipwrecked African slaves and Amerindians of the eastern Caribbean islands. The ancestral Garifuna revolted against British authorities on the island of St. Vincent and were expelled to the town of Punta Gorda on Roatán Island, Honduras, in 1797. There they established a community, thrived, and migrated along the coast to form communities in Belize, Guatemala, and Nicaragua; however, more than 80 percent of the Garifuna in Central America remain in Honduras.[12]

Physically similar to other Afro-Antilleans, the Garifuna regard themselves as culturally distinct.[13] They retain an Arawakan-derived language and important Amerindian cultural traditions including architecture. They also preserve African cultural traditions including dancing and drumming. Garifuna food culture blends the two heritages as well; they process bitter cassava to make *ereba,* the flat *casabe* bread, in a manner reminiscent of their South American Indian forbearers. They also prepare meals like *hudut* or *machuca* with mashed green plantains, coconut milk, and fish using methods similar to those found in West African cuisine. In an object example of their cultural synthesis, these foods are often served side by side.

Hudut

2 whole or filleted fish

6–8 green plantains

2 8-oz can coconut milk

2 tsp. black pepper

1 tsp. ground red pepper

salt to taste

Peel green plantains and boil in water for about 45 minutes. Remove from water and cool. Mash plantains until consistency matches mashed potatoes. Preseason fish with limejuice, pepper, and salt. Mix coconut milk and black pepper in deep frying pan at medium low heat. Simmer fish in coconut gravy, turning over repeatedly until done (usually 30–45 minutes). Serve large dollop of *hudut*; smother with plenty of gravy and fish.

OTHER IMMIGRANT GROUPS

Other immigrant influences in consumption patterns and production include the European and North American expatriates or retirees in the region. A much larger minority group includes Central Americans of Middle Eastern descent—Lebanese, Palestinians, Syrians, and Turks—who came to the region in several waves in the 1910s and 1920s and then again after 1948. Today well-established communities exist in the urban centers of Central American countries. Approximately 150,000 to 200,000 of Honduras's 6 million inhabitants for instance are of Middle Eastern descent. Sometimes disparagingly referred to as "Turcos," Middle Eastern Hondurans are prominent in business and commerce. Their traditional food culture is preserved in the home and in settings like the *Centro Social Hondureno Arabe*, a private country club located in the suburbs of San Pedro Sula, where Palestinian dishes like *falafil, kibbe*, and *baba ghanoush* are served alongside Honduran dishes such as beef filet with rice, beans, plantains, and tortillas.

Likewise, waves of immigration from Asia have also contributed to the diversity and complexity of urban centers and have consequently affected food tastes and consumption in various ways. In Panamá, for instance, there are between 135,000 and 200,000 ethnic Chinese. To feed and supply this ethnic market, restaurants and suppliers have arisen in Panamá City's two Chinatowns. In other major cities and towns of Nicaragua, Guatemala, Belize, and Costa Rica, there are Chinese restaurants, many of which make accommodations to local tastes and available produce in an additive manner. For instance an East Indian restaurant in Punta Gorda, Belize, serves palm heart tacari with breadfruit and fish, blending traditions and tastes of East and West. Belize also has a small German-speaking Mennonite population that emigrated from Mexico between 1958 and 1962 and who have contributed significantly to Belize's food economy by providing dairy and poultry to urban markets.[14] Communities of retired U.S. and Canadian citizens exist in Costa Rica, Guatemala, Honduras, Belize, and Panamá. Their influence on Central American food culture has been measured primarily through the introduction of and demand for globalized tastes and food practices.

INDEPENDENCE

The Spanish Empire was in slow decline from the 17th century onward, which meant increased autonomy for the colonial elite. When Mexico gained independence in 1821, the ruling classes from the five Central American provinces (Honduras, El Salvador, Nicaragua, and Costa Rica) were compelled to join the first Mexican Empire formed by Agustín de Ituribe. Within a year, a military coup ousted Ituribe and established a federal republic in Mexico. The five Central American provinces seceded to form their own state, the United Provinces of Central America. Panamá, having gained independence and joining in Gran Colombia, in 1819, was not included. The short-lived experiment in confederation collapsed after a civil war and fragmented in 1838 into the five separate republics known today. Over the next decades, the subject of unification or economic integration has been revisited more than 20 times, all ending in failure.

At the dawn of independence, Central America was sparsely populated. Out of a total of approximately 1 million people, most were indigenous (58%), another 37.5 percent were considered mestizo, a category that then included all persons of African descent, and a mere 45,000, or 4.5 percent, were considered Spaniards.[15] Independence meant among other things less interference from Spain and many Peninsulares returned to Spain. The caste system remained, however, and Criollos, or people of Spanish descent who were born in the Americas, ascended the social, political, and economic ladders. *Criollos* embraced a cultural identity shaped by both their Spanish roots and their American circumstance, but Central America retained deep divisions, cleaving people into classes with enduring differences in wealth, power, and prestige. The social hierarchy in Central America is actually older than the conquest. The Maya, too, had elite classes of nobles and priests who ruled over artisans, laborers, and slaves. The conquest did little to disrupt the indigenous system of hierarchy other than supplanting the top stratum and redirecting tribute payments to the church and Spanish lords. Today's status criteria recall the colonial past. Variables including skin color, ethnicity, credentials, occupation, residential area, language, and family pedigree all inform or determine one's position in the class system.[16] Likewise, dimensions of food culture may reflect or project a person's social standing, especially among the close-knit elite classes in Central America.

Elite Class

This socially distinct group typically includes only 2 to 5 percent of the population who draw power and wealth from various sources such as landownership, agriculture production and export, control of commercial enterprises, and government. In some countries, elites are a close-knit group of old families drawn together through kinship and association. In other societies, social mobility to elite status is possible, especially through education. At one time, upper class standing required among other things having "European" physical features, speech, and tastes, and thus consuming in the manner of the home country. The meals of upper class households in Central America were often studied, culinary replicas of the former European colonizers and heavily dependent on imported foods.[17] Today, elite consumption is still outwardly focused, but it is measured in higher levels of meat consumption, use of prepared foods, modern cooking appliances, and frequency of eating out and or employing cooks or housekeepers in the home.

Middle Class

Economic growth in the 20th century greatly expanded the middle classes. Beginning in Costa Rica, reformist and revolutionary political parties had emerged to challenge the continued rule of traditional elites. By the beginning of the 21st century, the size of the middle class varied across Central America, with 5 percent of the population belonging to the stratum in Nicaragua. At the other extreme in Costa Rica, most of the population consider themselves members of the middle class. More so than kinship, race, or ethnicity, membership in this group is defined by economic factors and occupation. The middle class encompasses entrepreneurs, tradesmen, professionals, teachers, technical personnel, and government administrators, including members of the military officer corps. Membership in this stratum is the most volatile, however, and is subject to downturns in the economy or political upheaval. Middle class Central Americans with the means often expatriate in difficult times. In terms of food culture, the middle classes are predictably mixed. Some with ambitions of upward mobility might emulate the norms and attitudes of the elite as was done in colonial times. Others, for reasons ranging from nostalgia to nationalism, eat in a manner more similar to the lower classes, albeit more regularly.

Lower Class

Most people in Central America are part of the lower social stratum. In addition to poverty, members of this class share limited access to health-care, sanitation, education, land, or other avenues for social mobility. In terms of livelihood, members of the lower class are employed as subsistence farmers and landless laborers attached to export agricultural production in the rural areas. Landlessness and unemployment in the rural areas have fostered a great influx of peasants to urban centers. In the urban areas, the lower class includes unskilled or semiskilled workers and, as there are also high rates of unemployment there as well, many people are dependent on the informal sector of the economy, working as market vendors, porters, or day laborers. The typical meals of the lower class in Central America are still affected by tradition and the legacies of colonial hierarchy. High levels of undernutrition prevail in Central America, particularly in parts of Guatemala, Nicaragua, and El Salvador. The typical meals of the lower classes are still based on beans and starches, such as rice, maize, and plantains, or root foods. Fresh fruit may be eaten occasionally, but normally little meat is eaten. In coastal areas, fish or seafood may be eaten occasionally.

THE MODERN ERA

Since the 16th century, Central America has been integrated in the world economy through an export-oriented agriculture with production centered on large monocrop plantations intended for markets in Spain. During the colonial period, indigo and cochineal were the principal exports. Over the years, there were cycles of boom and bust, but the market for them was finally wiped out by the development of synthetic dyes in the 1860s. Following their lot as colonies, the Central American republics continued to rely on export agriculture during the century after independence. The cultivation of cacao, coffee, and bananas in particular helped shape the character of the region for good or bad. Coffee and cacao were grown on upland volcanic soils in a variety of land tenure arrangements, usually at the expense of a more diversified agriculture. Likewise, banana cultivation, mostly controlled by foreign interests, also became important and were grown on sparsely inhabited land along the wide Atlantic coasts of Honduras, Guatemala, Costa Rica, and Panamá, later moving to the Pacific coasts after an outbreak of leaf spot disease.

The production of both commodities was facilitated greatly by innovations in transportation including the steamship and railroad and the involvement of U.S. government and private corporations on the isthmus. The U.S. government facilitated Panamanian independence in 1903, as well as the construction and operation of the Panamá Canal. An American entrepreneur, Minor Keith, constructed a transisthmus railroad in Costa Rica. Keith had bananas planted along the railroad rights of way for export to U.S. markets from Limón and thereby originated the United Fruit Company Subsequently, the United Fruit Company shaped the region's economy by developing ports, railroads, shipping, and other subsidiary interests. In turn the laborers drawn to the region especially from the West Indies, forever altered the ethnic and cultural composition of Central America.

Banana Republics

While bananas are an important food for Central Americans, their association with the region has created an ambivalent relationship with the fruit. Imported to the region by Spanish settlers, bananas were first grown commercially in Central America during the 1870s construction of the transnational railroad in Costa Rica. North American fruit companies, benefitted from favorable tax exemptions and other concessions from governments and cheap labor from the people, monopolized the banana business in Central America in short order. To ensure their market dominance, they employed various and unseemly methods including oppression of workers and the occasional regime change. The Central American economies of that era were characterized by poor infrastructures with heavy reliance on export agriculture and for this they came to be known mockingly as "Banana Republics." The term is attributed to the American writer and humorist, O. Henry, who set several short stories in a fictitious Central American country during his exile in Honduras.

In current usage, the term "banana republic" describes a generally unstable, despotic or otherwise backward regime, especially one where elections are fraudulent and corruption and cronyism is the norm. In a less critical sense, a banana republic can also mean a country where a large part of the economy is dominated by a single commodity. Banana Republics are vulnerable to economic fluctuation and high foreign debt, especially at times of low export prices or over-production and their politics are often controlled by foreign interests or private corporations.

For three decades after World War II, Central American economies grew as agricultural export production expanded to include sugarcane, cotton, oil palms, and most significant, cattle. The cattle economy, like bananas and coffee, transformed much of the landscape so that by the end of the 1980s, more than 9 million cattle were raised on 65 percent of the region's agricultural land. The conversion of forestland to pasture greatly accelerated environmental degradation, and ranching has led to a concentration of land resources into fewer hands and the dissociation of small holders from the land all across the region.

After the oil crisis of 1973, the Central American boom came to an abrupt stop and was followed by a protracted period of social and political turmoil and economic recession. The 1980s are sometimes referred to as the Lost Decade. Rural population growth, social injustice, and grinding poverty sparked open civil war and rebellion against governments in Nicaragua, Guatemala, and El Salvador. Military strongmen with repressive regimes emerged to lead Panamá and Honduras in the same era; only Belize and Costa Rica escaped directly, but even they suffered in the general miasma of the time. The wars gravely affected the social frameworks across the region. A large part of the population suffered from hunger, especially those in the lower social strata. Millions of people were displaced from their homes either to relocate in refugee camps or to flee the country all together along with the capital, skills, and talents needed to sustain a thriving culture. Agricultural production fell and caloric intake decreased as did illness, malnutrition, and undernutrition. Governments had fewer resources with which to address education, public health, and disease prevention.

The 1990s was a decade of generally moderate economic recovery, aided by internal policy reforms. Central America emerged from the Lost Decade optimistic and hopeful that peace would spread and take hold but also deeply in debt. It is expected that the recovery in living standards, losses to health, education, and capital investment will take years to realize. The turnaround thus far has seen a general improvement in the economic conditions and a host of structural adjustments. In 2005, Costa Rica, Dominican Republic, El Salvador, Guatemala, Honduras, Nicaragua, and the United States became signatories to the Central American Free Trade Agreement (CAFTA), a trade agreement modeled on NAFTA that took effect on January 1, 2006. CAFTA aims to eliminate tariffs and trade barriers and effectively open borders and markets to the importation and export of foodstuffs. Central American consumers hope they will enjoy greater access to a better diversity and quality of foods. Recent concern has been expressed over the effect of the agreement on rural food producers who may be negatively affected by cheap food imports.

Throughout Central America, postwar political stability has also fostered a rush of outsiders seeking diversions on the pristine beaches, Maya ruins, and virgin rainforests. Tourism expanded rapidly and enormously in the 1990s and now represents the second largest source of foreign revenue in Belize and Guatemala and the largest in Costa Rica. Resorts and other tourist destinations are already of major importance in the region. Ecotourism in particular is of growing significance and has laid the groundwork for culinary tourism in the region.

NOTES

1. Gordon R. Willey, "The 'Intermediate Area' of Nuclear America: Its Prehistoric Relationships to Middle America and Peru." In *Actas del XXXIII Internacional de Americanistas* 1 (1959): 184–94.

2. *The Maya: Diego de Landa's Account of the Affairs of the Yucatan*, trans. and ed. A. R. Pagden. (Chicago: J. Philip O'Hara, 1975).

3. William M. Denevan, *The Native Population of the Americas in 1492*. (Madison: University of Wisconsin Press, 1976).

4. M. W. Helms, *Asang: Adaptations to Culture Contact in a Miskito Community* (Gainesville: University of Florida Press, 1971).

5. Bernard Nietschman, "Hunting and Fishing Focus Among the Miskito Indians, Eastern Nicaragua," *Human Ecology* 1, no. 1 (1972): 41–67.

6. Alfonso Vila Rojas, "The Maya of Yucatán," in *Handbook of Middle American Indians*. Vol. 7, *Ethnology*, ed. Evon Z. Vogt (Austin: University of Texas Press, 1969), pp. 24–75.

7. Sophie D. Coe, *America's First Cuisines* (Austin: University of Texas Press, 1994), pp. 145–64.

8. Alfred W. Crosby, *The Columbian Exchange: Biological and Cultural Consequences of 1492*, 30th Anniv. Ed. (Westport CT: Greenwood Press, 2003).

9. Adrian Recinos, *Pedro De Alvarado, Conquistador De Mexico y Guatemala* (Mexico, D. F, Mexico: Panuco, Fondo De Cultura Economica, 1952).

10. Used with permission from the Antigua Cooking School, Antiqua, Guatemala, 2008

11. CIA Factbook 2008, https://www.cia.gov/library/publications/ the-world-factbook/geos.

12. Peter H. Herlihy, "Central American Indian Peoples and Lands Today," in *Central America: A Natural and Cultural Area*, ed. Anthony G. Coates (New Haven: Yale University Press, 1997), pp. 215–40.

13. Michael R. McDonald, "Learning Island Food culture, Tasting Ethnographic Methods," in Anthropological Notebooks: Journal of the Slovenian Anthropological Society. Contributions to Anthropology of Food and Eating 12, no. 1 (2006).

14. Richard Wilk, Home Cooking in the Global Village. Caribbean Food from Buccaneers to Ecotourists (Oxford, UK: Berg Publishers, 2006), pp. 147–48.

15. Julio César Pinto Soria, *Raíces históricas del Estado en Centro América* (Guatemala City: Editorial Universitaria de Guatemala, 1980).

16. Kevin A. Yelvington, "Patterns of 'Race,' Ethnicity, Class, and Nationalism," in *Understanding Contemporary Latin America*, 3rd ed., ed. Richard S. Hillman (Boulder: Lynne Rienner Publications, 2005), pp. 237–71.

17. Paul Kirchhoff, "Mesoamérica," *Acta Americana* 1 (1943): 92–107.

2

Major Foods and Ingredients

Any discussion of Central American foods must begin with an obligatory bow to a trio of staple foods: corn (hereafter maize), rice, and beans. The ubiquitous meal of rice and beans now synonymous with Latin cuisine is found and favored in all of Central America and known by a variety of names: *moros y cristianos, casamiento,* and *gallo pinto* to name a few. Local custom dictates the type of beans, whether they are cooked together with the rice or apart, is what constitutes an appropriate additive and how and when the pairing is presented, but it is generally accompanied by tortillas, typically made from maize flour.

RICE (*ORYZA SATIVA*)

The Moors first introduced rice to Spain more than 1,000 years ago, and subsequently rice was introduced to Central America by the Spanish after the conquest. Today, rice is commonly grown along coastal regions in all countries of the region. Compared to its neighbors in the Caribbean region, where per capita consumption is 105 pounds per year, Central American rice consumption is a low 40 pounds per person.[1] This number masks further internal variation. Consumption of rice varies across the landscape in nearly inverse relation to maize consumption. The highest annual per capita consumption of rice is around 132 pounds in Panamá and Costa Rica, tapering to 11 pounds per person annually in Guatemala. In all countries, consumption outpaces production, necessitating the importation of rice, primarily from the United States, where per capita annual consumption of rice is 18 pounds.

White rice is preferred and cooks commonly soak or rinse the rice before cooking to remove excess starch. It is then sautéed in oil with onions until lightly puffed and toasted. Water is then added, with a little salt to taste. Well-prepared rice is tender, dry, and grainy, not mushy. Rice is typically paired with beans as a main meal or side dish such as *gallo pinto*, the national dish of Costa Rica. *Arroz con pollo* is a favorite dish throughout the region from Guatemala to Panamá. Dishes similar to Spanish paellas abound, combining local seafood with rice and often substituting *achiote* for saffron to provide the coloring. Rice is also used in making desserts and the refreshing beverage *horchata*.

Horchata (Rice Water or Rice Milk)

Approximately 4 servings

1 cup uncooked white rice

1/4 cup ground, blanched almonds or almond meal

1 cinnamon stick

6 cups water, divided

1/2 tsp. vanilla extract

1/2 cup sugar

Place rice, almonds, and cinnamon in a blender or food processor. (Use a *metate y mano* if you want the authentic experience!) Process until ground to a fine powder. Place mixture in large bowl or saucepan. Add water and mix well. Cover and let cool in refrigerator for five to eight hours. When beverage is chilled, return to blender and process for a few seconds to homogenize. Strain mixture through cheese cloth or filter into large bowl or pitcher. Discard rice dregs, return liquid to blender, add sugar and vanilla. To serve, pour over ice in tall glasses.

BEANS

Beans are a truly indigenous food. Domestication began more than 7,000 years ago in Central America likely first as weeds along the edges of root crop gardens and then growing in importance over the millennia to become one of the most important foods in the region and the world. In 2003, the average per capita consumption of beans in Central America was 24 pounds.[2] Consumption does vary across the region and by socioeconomic status, but the beans consumed in Central America fall within four species: *Phaseolus lunatus* (lima beans), *Phaseolus coccineus* (runner beans), *Phaseo-*

lus acutifolious (tepary bean), and *Phaseolus vulgaris* or common bean. The term *common bean* actually subsumes even greater variety: the black turtle bean, navy or epa bean, red kidney, pinto, great northern, marrow, and yellow eye are all common beans, as are the edible pods of snap beans and string beans. As noted, leguminous climbing beans are planted along with maize all over the Americas. For their part, the beans fix nitrogen in the soils, which supplement nutrient uptake by the maize plants, which provide stalks for the beans to climb. In a similar way, beans and maize work together in the diet to an important degree. Maize is high in starch but deficient in certain proteins, specifically the amino acids tryptophan and lysine, whereas beans have high protein content and generous amounts of dietary fiber, complex carbohydrates, and other dietary essentials. The combination of beans and grain foods (maize, wheat, or rice) provides complementary nutrition, especially for people in Central America who consume little or no meat. All beans, however, are not equal in the eyes of the beholder. Consumers in Costa Rica and Guatemala strongly prefer black beans, whereas consumers in El Salvador, Honduras, and Nicaragua have a marked preference for the small red beans.

MAIZE *(ZEA MAYS)*

Maize, known as corn in North America, is a food with varying importance in Central America. At one time it was the primary food source of all sedentary peoples in Mesoamerica. As maize is a particularly fertile and nutritious plant, it is arguably the foundation on which pre-Columbian societies were built. Maize is incorporated in Maya mythology, art forms, and various religious rituals that continue to the present. In Guatemala and El Salvador, people still consume a lot of maize, averaging 10 ounces of maize per day). In Honduras and Nicaragua, consumption is somewhat less, about 5 and 6 ounces per day, respectively, but high enough to reveal its considerable dietary significance.[3] Over the past several decades, maize has become markedly less important in the outer reaches of Central America. Daily per capita consumption of maize in Panamá is 2 ounces and less than half an ounce per person in Costa Rica. Maize plays a lesser role in Belizean cuisine as well where per capita consumption has been falling for decades and is now around 1 ounce per day.[4] These differences mark recent changes in which other foods have become more readily available. They also reflect the evolution of Central American food culture toward more pronounced regional characteristics and identity.

One measure of maize's important legacy in the region is found in the diversity of culinary uses to which the grain has been put. Fresh ears of

Dried maize. AP Photo/Esteban
Felix.

maize known as *elotes* are usually sold steaming hot on a stick by street
vendors throughout Central America. They are roasted or boiled then
smeared with various toppings including butter, salt, limejuice, and chile
powder.

A more involved preparation of maize involves boiling and soaking
dried maize in a calcium oxide solution (see Chapter 3) and then grinding
to form a soft dough called masa. Prepared masa flour is widely available
and used to make tortilla, the flat bread usually present in daily meals.
Tortillas are cooked on a hot *comal* or griddle, lightly scorched, and served
still warm. In Guatemala and points east, tortillas are smaller and somewhat thicker than the Tex-Mex version more familiar to North American
consumers. Central American tortillas are more similar in size and shape
to silver dollar pancakes. In El Salvador, people do eat tortillas but generally prefer *pupusas* (also known as *arepas*), small, thick cakes of maize,
often filled with cheese or meat, for their daily bread.

Tamales made from maize are popular throughout the region and are
prepared in a variety of ways. The word *tamal* comes from the Nahuatl language and means "wrapped food." Tamales consist of ground, dried maize
flour or the raw mashed kernels, moistened into a dough, shaped into

thick, rectangular pieces that are filled with different vegetables or meats, or simply sweetened with milk and sugar. The tamales are then wrapped in cornhusks, avocado leaves, or banana leaves and then steamed or boiled. Tamales can be eaten on any occasion, but in some countries, such as El Salvador, Costa Rica, and Panamá, they are generally prepared for holidays. The neat packages of corn meal are also the original travelers' food.

As with tortilla, each region has a variation on the tamale; for example, in both Honduras and Nicaragua, a distinction is drawn between *tamales*, which are wrapped in husks and *nacatamales*, which are wrapped in banana or plantain leaves. In El Salvador, tamales proper are different from *tamales rellenos*, which are similar to the Honduran and Nicaraguan *nacatamales*. Another way of using ground maize is as a thickener for stews or for giving a distinctive flavoring to certain dishes. Ground maize can also be toasted and used to flour meats or fish for deep frying.

Finally, maize is also the ingredient for many traditional Central American beverages. *Atoles* are drinks made from masa, water, *piloncillo* (brown sugar), cinnamon, and vanilla. An *atol* is typically served hot or warm and has a thick gruel-like consistency. *Shuco* is a special type of *atol* made from a base of blue maize and various other ingredients. Other regional variants on the maize beverage include *chilate* from western Honduras and El Salvador. Ground cacao seeds and *achiote* (annatto seeds) are added to the basic *atol* mixture to make *chilate*. Yet another beverage is *pinolillo* where water and sugar are added to toasted ground maize flour and chocolate to make this national beverage of Nicaragua. Consumption of *pinolillo* is so widespread that it has become a symbol of Nicaraguan culture, and some Nicaraguans refer to themselves as *Pinoleros*. As Central American food culture gains its identity through metatezation, it necessarily includes foods from diverse origins. The following foods are organized first into dietary categories and then further identified for their particular New World or Old World origins.

VEGETABLES

Various terms are used to describe the roots, rhizomes, leaves, and flowers that are eaten as a part of Central American cuisine. Vegetables are eaten in soups and savory stews, as well as simple side dishes and salads.

New World Roots and Tubers

More than 700,000 tons of root foods are consumed annually in the seven countries of Central America.[5] Some species do have edible leaves, but the distinguishing physical feature is the fleshy underground storage organ that is abundant in starch or sugar and low in protein and oil. In contemporary Central American cuisine, root crops are a useful source of calories and complement other foods.

Cassava (Manihot esculenta)

Commonly known in Central America as yuca, manioc, or tapioca, cassava is a shrubby perennial species of the lowland tropics believed to have originated as a cultivated plant either in Central America or in northern South America.[6] Small-scale farmers using traditional methods on marginal lands that are not well suited to other crops typically grow cassava. The plant is propagated by planting stakes cut from the woody stems of mature plants into raised mounds of earth. While young leaves are edible, the roots are sought as an important staple food throughout the region. Because fresh cassava roots deteriorate rapidly (within three to four days) after harvesting, they are usually consumed immediately or processed into a form that has better storage characteristics. The presence of hydrocyanic glucosides (HCN) in all plant parts presents some problems for consumers. Cassava is categorized as either "sweet" when low levels of HCN are present, or "bitter" to signify higher, even toxic levels of HCN. Sweet varieties require no special pretreatment before consumption. The heat from cooking suffices in detoxifying the root. The Garifuna people of Honduras and Belize produce the bitter varieties and, following a technique developed in the Northwest Amazon, make them edible by shredding, soaking, and squeezing in a basketry sleeve known as a *ruguma* and then cooking to rid them of their toxicity. Cassava is consumed in a variety of ways; the whole root may be peeled and boiled or chopped for inclusion in soups and stews. In many parts of Central America, the cooked roots are ground into dough and then patted into thin flat cakes and cooked on the *comal* to make cassava bread known in Spanish as *pan de casabe*.

Potato (Solanum tuberosum)

The potato, a tuber of South American origin, is the most successful of the New World cultigens, based on its enormous popularity the world over. The starchy, tuberous potato known as *papas* or *patatas* in Spanish, likely derived from the Taino term *batata* for sweet potato. Potatoes are a perennial plant of the Solanaceae (Nightshade) family and are related to the tomato, pepper, and eggplant. Potatoes have been cultivated for at least 2,400 years. Recent scholarly publications have narrowed the site of domestication to an area in Peru, just north of Lake Titicaca.[7] Through trade and conquest, the crop likely diffused throughout adjacent areas of Central America where it was adapted to local conditions and was introduced to Europe in the 1570s after the conquest of Peru by the Spanish. Like other tubers, potatoes are consumed throughout Central America in stews and in baked, fried, roasted, and boiled forms. As elsewhere, potato chips are popular as a snack food.

Yam (Dioscoreaceae spp.)

Yam is an English derivative of an African word *nyami*, referring to the starchy, edible root of the *Dioscorea* plants. Hundreds of species of *dioscorea* tubers are produced and consumed in the world today, and many appear to have been domesticated independently in the Old and New Worlds. In Central America they are known by various common names including *ñame*, *cush cush*, and *yampi*. Not to be confused with the sweet potato, which is erroneously called yam or Louisiana yam in North American parlance, true yams are climbing perennial vines with heart-shaped leaves. Often grown on trellises, the plant produces underground tubers that vary in size and shape, averaging 3 to 8 pounds but sometimes reaching 40 pounds or more, with white or yellow somewhat fibrous flesh. Yams are typically treated like potatoes and cassava in Central American cuisine. Although consumption of yams is negligible in most Central American countries, the tubers are favored in Panamá and Costa Rica where daily per capita consumption is less than half an ounce.[8]

Sweet Potato (Ipomoea batatas)

The sweet potato is a native plant of the Americas, with archaeological evidence of its cultivation dating back 10,000 years in coastal Peru. This tuber was famously encountered by Christopher Columbus and his shipmates and was thereafter carried to Europe, Africa, and points beyond by explorers and colonizers. Evidence of the sweet potato in Polynesia suggests that contact between the Pacific and the America's predates European arrival and that the sweet potato was among the first truly global foods.[9] The white sweet potato with drier, white flesh and pink or brown and white skin is known as *boniato* or *camote*. The main differences between the white-fleshed and the familiar orange-fleshed sweet potatoes are that the white-fleshed types are usually less sweet, generally grow to a larger size, and have variable root shape. Sweet potatoes and the true yams (various *Dioscorea* species), however, are from very different plant families and are easily distinguishable by shape and taste.

Jicama (Pachyrhizus erosus)

Also known as *yacon* or the yam bean, jicama is another native tuber of the Americas. Its skin is thin and can be gray, tan, or brown. Also, it has a short root and contains white flesh with a clean, crunchy crispness that is set off by a refreshing sweetness. Raw jicama has a flavor that is similar to a pear or apple and is eaten fresh with limejuice or chile powder condiments. It also has a juicy texture and does not discolor when left out in the open air for a while. Because of this quality, raw jicama is often used as an accompaniment to other raw vegetables. When jicama is used in cooking, it tends to take on the flavors of the ingredients with which it is combined. Common uses for jicama include eating it raw or adding it raw to slaws or salads such as to a kiwi-orange fruit salad or to a *ceviche*.

Jicama and Maize (Corn) Salad

4 cups corn (use canned, frozen, or freshly cooked)

1 large jicama (1.5–2 lbs), washed, peeled, and diced

3 large mangos, peeled and diced

1 cup chopped red onion

1/2 cup chopped fresh cilantro

1/4 cup chopped sweet red pepper

1/2 cup limejuice

salt and red chile pepper to taste

In a large serving bowl, combine the corn kernels, jicama, mango, red onion, and cilantro. Pour the lime juice over and season with chile, salt and pepper. Toss until well blended. Let sit for an hour or more covered with plastic wrap. *¡buen provecho!*

Malanga and Dasheens (Xanthosoma and Colocasia)

Malanga, also called *quequisque*, *yautia*, *cocoyam*, or *tannia*, is a plant in the Arum Lily family and a significant part of the pre-Columbian diet of highland Central America. Its more popular cousin, the *taro* or *dasheen*, is from the genus *Colocasia* that originates in the Old World and is the famed source of poi in Polynesia. Malanga and taro are often confused and called by each other's names, perhaps because the plants grow side-by-side in gardens and look and taste the same in the cooking pot. These two potato-like vegetables are not true tubers but rather corms. The edible portion of the plant is a corm or a group of small corms or cormels found underground, although the leaves of several species are also eaten as green vegetables. The skins are usually brown; the flesh ranges in color from white to yellow to purple, and they are cooked in various ways. Most are boiled, steamed, or fried in oil. Like other root vegetables, they can also be cut into small chunks and added to stews or soups. The young leaves of some varieties are also used as an important green vegetable throughout the tropics.

Root Vegetables from Abroad

In part because of native abundance, few root vegetables from abroad have been incorporated into the Central American pantry with these notable exceptions.

Carrots (Daucus carota L)

The Arabs are credited with introducing carrots to Spain, who in turn passed them along to the New World. Carrots are commonly consumed raw in salads or as crudités in special dishes such as the *fiambre*. Less frequently, they are eaten cooked and then generally added to soups or *cocidos* (stews).

Onions (Allium cepa)

Really a bulb and not a tuber, onions are one of the oldest vegetables known to humankind and are found in almost all of the world's food cultures. Onions arrived early on in the conquest and have been incorporated readily into Central American food production and preparation. Onions are usually chopped or sliced and added to many types of dishes including sauces, salads, and *cocidos* and as a garnish in traditional dishes like *guacamol*.

Gourds, Squashes, and Pumpkins

When pumpkins and squashes were first brought back to Spain, the entire family of cucurbits was given the collective name *calabaza*, a word of Arabic origin meaning "gourd" and a label that persists. Some taxonomic confusion remains, but one can generally distinguish among the various cucurbits primarily by their uses in Central American foodways and by the names such as *zapallo*, *ayote*, *auyama*, and *calabacin*, all commonly used to describe these fruits.

Gourds (Lagenaria siceraria)

Gourds are unlike other cucurbits in that they are grown for their material properties such as the hard outer shell or fiber rather than food value. Bottle gourds, for instance, are one of the oldest known domesticates and have been used in the Americas for 10,000 years or more as dippers and containers.

Summer Squash (Cucurbita pepo)

Summer squashes referenced in popular accounts and academic studies are the zucchini and yellow squashes known in Spanish as *zapallo*, *calabacitas*, or *calabacines*. Summer squash fruits are harvested immature, have a short storage life, and are used in soups and sauces or as fillings as are the lush egg-yolk colored flowers, which are also used in soups or fillings for quesadillas in some Central American dishes.

Winter Squash (Cucurbita moschata)

Varieties of hard-skinned squashes such as butternut, acorn, or spaghetti squashes are known as "winter" squash for their ability to be stored for several weeks or months before consumption. In Central America they are known variously as *ayote*, *auyama*, *zapallito*, or *calabaza*. Winter squash fruits have many different shapes and colors and an inedible peel, which distinguishes them from summer varieties. The flesh is fine-grained and is eaten ripe, and winter squashes are the best choice for baking and as additives to soups and stews. Winter squashes with round, orange fruit, referred to as pumpkins in English, are known by various Spanish names including *ayote* and *zapallo*. Pumpkins are grown both in maize fields (*milpas*) and vegetable gardens, as well as in other more intensive systems. The fruits are harvested at full seed maturity but generally do not store as well as other winter squash types. As the flesh is generally a little too coarse and strong-flavored for eating, most pumpkins are harvested for their seeds. Roasted pumpkin or *pepitas* are eaten as a snack food, used as a garnish for soups and salads, and form the important base ingredient for *pepián* sauces in the signature dishes of Guatemala.

Chayote (Sechium edule)

Chayote is an interesting one-seeded fruit in the gourd family. It comes from a climbing, perennial vine and is native to tropical America. It is also known as vegetable pear, *mirliton, christophene, güisquilles,* or *chou-chou.* This pumpkin was a dietary staple for both the Maya and Aztec civilizations. Chayote has a mild taste, similar to a cucumber or zucchini squash, and is eaten in similar fashion.

LEAFY VEGETABLES

Native

Chaya (Cnidoscolus chayamansa)

Chaya is a little known leafy green vegetable of dry regions of the tropics. The name comes from the Mayan *chay.* Other common names are tree spinach, *chaya col, kikilchay,* and *chaykeken.* Younger leaves and stems are cut and used much like spinach. Large leaves are cut into manageable pieces before cooking. Leaves are immersed and simmered for 20 minutes and then served with oil or butter. *Chaya* is a good source of protein, vitamins, calcium, and iron. Raw *chaya* leaves, however, are highly poisonous, but a few minutes of boiling destroys most of the toxin.

From Abroad

Cabbage (Brassica olereacea)

Current botanical evidence points to the eastern Mediterranean and Asia Minor as the place of origin of cabbage. Now well established in Central America, raw cabbage is usually sliced into thin strips or shredded for use in salads. Because of its naturally mild spicy flavor, cabbage is also used to make *curtido,* the traditional topping for Salvadoran *pupusas. Curtido* is usually allowed to ferment slightly at room temperature before serving, becoming a kind of Salvadoran sauerkraut. A similar dish is known as *ensalada de repollo* in Nicaragua.

Lettuce (Lactuca sativa)

Various types of lettuce are widely grown as an export crop for North American markets. Lettuce has also gained a place in the Central American food culture with the now popular custom of eating an *ensalada fresca* (fresh salad), which usually includes a mix of fresh tomatoes, cucumber, and lettuce as a part of the mid-day meal.

FRUITS

The great abundance of fruits in Central America provides people with a year-round resource not enjoyed by people in more temperate climes. Many Old World fruit species also favor the Central American climate and thrive alongside the native species. Most fruits are eaten fresh as snacks, but there are as many recipes for including fruits into desserts, beverages, and main courses as there are fruits themselves. Some important Central American fruits are discussed here; however, there are countless others.

Native Fruits

Avocado (Persea americana)

Avocados, members the laurel family, were cultivated as far back as 9000 B.C.E. The Spanish name *aguacate* is derived from the word *ahuacatl*, meaning testicle in the Nahuatl language. Perhaps because of their evocative shape, avocados have had a longstanding reputation as an aphrodisiac. The fruit may be rough or smooth-skinned, and green or black in color.

Cherimoya (Annona cherimola)

The cherimoya is an unusual looking but delicious fruit believed to be indigenous to the Andean mountain valleys of South America. Also known as custard apple in English-speaking countries, cherimoya is now commonly grown in temperate areas of Costa Rica and other countries of Central America. The cherimoya's skin is deep green, with small, soft spines covering the surface, along with geometric scallop grooves. When ripe, the fruit turns greenish yellow and becomes much softer. The flesh is white and juicy with a highly aromatic vanilla-like flavor. The cherimoya is most commonly eaten out of hand or scooped with a spoon. The cherimoya is of the Annona family with many closely related tropical American fruits such as the *guanábana* or *soursop* (A. *muricata*) and the sugar apple (A. *squamosa*), which are also enjoyed across the region.

Guava (Psidium guajava)

A Peruvian native, the guava was already established in Mexico at the time of the Hispanic conquest. Known as *guayaba* in Spanish, guavas grow on a small tree and have large smooth-edged leaves and white flowers from which develop somewhat pear-shaped fruits. Guava fruits vary in size and color, ranging from pale green through yellow to (sometimes) scarlet when ripe. The flesh also varies in color from creamy-white to bright pink. The inner section of the fruit is scattered with gritty little seeds in a circular pattern around the core. The large, pale-fleshed, pear-shaped guavas are considered the best for eating, and smaller, pink-fleshed varieties such as the strawberry guava are used in the preparation of jellies and guava paste.

Jocotes (Spondias purpurea)

Jocotes are small, very juicy, green and orange fruits whose name derives from the Indian word *xotoci*. They are in season from August to October and are commonly found in markets or roadside stands. In Costa Rica, *jocotes* are also boiled in a brown sugar syrup and water then served cold with sour cream.

Mamoncillo (Melicoccus bijugatus)

The small, oval green-colored fruit is known by various names including *mamon*, *genip*, *ginep*, *guenepa*, and Spanish lime and is a favorite of children all over Central America and the Caribbean Islands. This fruit typically grows in clusters of 12 or more from a single stem. It is similar in shape and size to a large green olive; the outer flesh of the fruit is thin and brittle. The skin is traditionally cracked by the teeth and peeled away to expose a coral to cream-colored flesh. The tart, tangy pulp of the fruit is sucked by putting the whole fruit inside the mouth; afterward the seed and skin are discarded. Despite the light color of the fruit's flesh, the juice stains a dark brown color.

Papaya (Carica papaya)

Another important Central American fruit is the papaya whose name originates in the Carib language and was adopted and diffused via Spanish speakers throughout the region. Papaya is also known variously as the tree melon, *fruta bomba*, *lechosa*, or pawpaw. There are varieties of the fruit with differing size, taste, and color. The fruits are ripe when soft like a ripe avocado, and the taste is similar to a mild pineapple and peach, without the tartness and with a texture of slightly over-ripened cantaloupe. The ripe fruit is usually eaten raw, without the skin or seeds. The unripe green fruit of papaya can be eaten cooked, usually in salads, stews, and in a specialty dish of Costa Rica, *Picadillo de Papaya verde*. The flesh of the mature green papaya is very high in papain, an enzyme that is used in a dried form to tenderize meat.

Passion Fruit (Passiflora dulis)

This climbing herb is native to South America but is found now throughout the region and is a popular ornamental plant. Its name refers to the passion of Christ because the flower's five petals are reminiscent of the crown of thorns placed on Jesus at the Crucifixion. The actual passion fruit looks a little bit like a plum, but the edible part is a seed kernel surrounded by a mucilaginous jelly.

Pejibayes (Bactris gasipaes)

Reddish-yellow fruits of pejibaye palm known also as peach palm fruit are often sold in markets and by vendors at tables along the roads. Edible only after boiling, pejibayes are served often in popular *sopa de pejibaye*. The pulp is similar to avocado in texture and tastes something more like pumpkin.

Pineapple (Ananas comosus)

The pineapple plant is a bromeliad with long, pointed, straplike leaves. The pineapple fruit is egg-shaped, of varying sizes, with flattened bottom and a tough, waxy rind made up of hexagonal units. It ranges in color from dark green, to orange-yellow or reddish when the fruit is ripe. The flesh, too, ranges in color from nearly white to yellow. Originally domesticated by the Guarani Indians of northern Paraguay, the pineapple became important throughout the Americas as it was diffused up through South and Central America to Mexico and the West Indies long before the arrival of Europeans.

Pineapples do not ripen until after they have been picked, so they must be harvested at the peak of freshness for best flavor. The flesh of the fruit is cut up in various ways and eaten fresh in salads, pulverized in to juice, or cooked in pies, cakes, puddings, or made into sauces or preserves. In Panamá, very small pineapples are cut from the plant with a few inches of stem to serve as a handle; the rind is removed except at the base; and the flesh is eaten out of hand like corn on the cob. Pineapple juice contains high concentrations of bromelain, an enzyme that is used in a way similar to papain, which is extracted from papaya to tenderize meats.

Pitaya (Hylocereus polyrhizus)

The pitaya or dragon fruit is native to Central and South America and is known best for its unusual appearance. Pitaya are one of the most widely distributed members of the cactus family. This epiphyte produces flowers at the end of vines, which later become high-quality fruits that resemble those of the prickly pear but without the spines. Fruits can weigh up to 10 ounces and contain small, black seeds. The fruit flesh can be white, red, or magenta depending on the variety. The red-fleshed varieties contain lycopene, a natural antioxidant also found in tomatoes that is known to fight cancer and heart disease, and to lower blood pressure. Pitaya are believed to have antianemic characteristics as well. Despite the health benefits and its spectacular appearance, the fruit has gone virtually unnoticed for centuries. Pitaya fruit is mostly used for creating rather thick juices (often enriched with some lemon juice), but the fruit's flesh can also be eaten plain (cut into small pieces) or in fruit salads.

Sapodilla (Manilkara zapota van royen)

The sapodilla tree native to Central America produces this egg-shaped, tasty fruit, as well as a sap once used in the production of chewing gum. The outer brown, rough-textured skin of the fruit covers amber to brown-colored juicy and fragrant flesh containing small black, inedible seeds. Spicy sweet in flavor, the orange to dark reddish-brown flesh has a vanilla-flavored meat with taste and textures similar to banana. Sapodillas vary in size, but are usually less than four inches in diameter. This fruit is also known as a *black zapote, nispero, sapodillo* and *zapotilla*. Sapodillas can be eaten fresh, served in salads, scooped out and served in a bowl; as an ingredient for cakes, sweet breads, custards, blended fruit drinks, flavored ices; or served pureed and made into sauces and dressings for fish or poultry.

Sapote (Pouteria sapota)

The sapote tree originates in Central America, and different varieties can be found throughout the region. The term is believed to be derived from the Aztec word *tzapotl*, a general term applied to all soft, sweet fruits.

There is a confusing list of vernacular names including *colorado, mamey, mamey sapote, mamey rojo, mammee apple, or red sapote.*[10] Sapote trees produce fruits year-round, although the peak season occurs from April to August. Sapote is in the same family as the sapodilla fruit, but the sapote fruit is larger. It has an oval shape and can measure up to 7 inches in diameter. The rind is thick and has a reddish coffee color. The pulp, which is red or orange, is soft and sweet and there are two long, black seeds inside. Typically it can be eaten by itself right out of the rind, and the inner part of the seed can be used for making various confectioneries.

Tomatillos (Physalis philadelphica)

The tomatillo (*Physalis philadelphica*) is a smallish vine-fruit about the size of a medium egg. The tomatillo is native to Mexico and Guatemala and is similar in appearance and culinary role to the tomato. Various names link tomatillo to its namesake: *tomate de cascara, tomate verde, tomate de fresadilla, miltomates,* and the husk tomato in English, because the fruit is enclosed in a papery outer skin. Tomatillos have not enjoyed the international popularity of their red-skinned cousins and have remained a fairly regional food, unknown to many outside Central America. Various archaeological findings reveal the use of tomatillo in pre-Columbian times, and it has remained a component of the Mexican and Guatemalan diet up to the present. When green, the fruit is tart but becomes yellow and sweeter as it ripens. The fruit of the tomatillo is used raw or prepared for marinades, purees, or as an element in chile sauces known as *salsas verde* (green sauces) to which it contributes glutinous texture and lemony flavor. Tomatillos are also used to impart flavor to white rice and to tenderize red meats.

Tomatoes (Solanum lycopersicum or Lycoperiscon esculentum)

Tomatoes are among the most important food crops in all parts of the world. Botanically considered a berry for its firm skin, seeds, and cavity filled with mucus-like substance, the first tomatoes were likely small red and yellow berry-size fruits in coastal South America. Wild ancestors of today's tomatoes, they spread north several thousand years before the Spanish exploration and were domesticated and cultivated throughout the expanse of Central America by the time of the arrival of the first conquistadors. Like so many New World foods, tomatoes have achieved far greater acceptance and popularity outside Mesoamerica, becoming synonymous with the cuisines of various southern European countries. Per capita consumption of tomatoes in Italy for instance is more than 132 pounds per person annually. Tomatoes are still consumed in their ancestral homeland, but they play more of a complementary role to the food culture of Central America where annual per capita consumption ranges from than 3.5 pounds per person in Nicaragua and Honduras to 30 pounds per person in El Salvador.[11]

Fruits from Abroad

Bananas and Plantains (Musa spp)

The word banana is a general term embracing a number of species or hybrids in the genus *Musa* of the family Musaceae. Bananas do not actually grow on trees but rather on herbaceous plants on which fruit grows in hanging clusters known as a hand, with 3 to 20 hands forming a bunch. Bananas were first carried to the New World early in the 16th century by Portuguese mariners who transported the plant from the West African coast to South America. Secondary diffusion and subsequent waves of settlers brought them to Central America where they were quickly incorporated into small-scale production. Today Central Americans consume on average 33 pounds of bananas per year.[12] Several varieties of banana

Banana harvesting, Costa Rica. AP Photo/ Kent Gilbert.

are found including red bananas and the *manzano* or apple banana. These four-inch long fruits are sweet yet have a slight tartness and are compared to a cross between an apple and a very sweet banana.

Most North American consumers refer to the yellow fruits consumed fresh as *banana* and reserve the term *plantain* for the larger, more angular fruits intended for cooking. The distinction in Central America is not that clear, however, and the terms may even be reversed in some locales. Bananas are known by various names in banana-growing areas including *banano*, *platano macho*, *cambur*, and *guineo*, but the terms refer generally to the sweet "dessert" fruit that are usually eaten raw.

Plantains or *plátanos* in Spanish are members of the same family as bananas. They are typically much larger than bananas and are not palatable as a raw fruit. When green (*verde*), plantains are boiled and are usually served as a starchy vegetable to accompany meat, poultry, or fish. Green plantains are also thinly sliced and deep-fried and are served as a snack similar to potato chips. The slices are thick before they are fried, and right after finishing the frying, they are flattened to a width of around 1/2 inch. They are then fried again until crispy. These flat but thick plantain chips are served with salt or lime. Slicing them lengthwise is another option (fried plantains in this shape are called *tajadas*). When ripe (*maduro*), plantain skins become blotchy or completely black. They are fried and are sometimes mashed in a favorite recipe of the Garifuna, *machuca de platanos*, or seasoned mashed plantains.

Citrus

A number of citrus fruits are produced and consumed in Central America and play an important part in defining the food culture. Sweet and sour oranges, lemons, and limes were all brought to the Americas after the conquest. Two of the more popular citrus fruits in Central American foodways are limes and oranges.

Limes

(*Citrus aurantifolia*) are small citrus fruits that are usually harvested green; they are a common food used mostly for the juice that is used to impart a sour and refreshing fragrance to cold and warm dishes and drinks. Limejuice is highly aromatic and therefore preferred over lemon juice. One popular Central American dish that makes special use of limejuice is ceviche in which raw fish is marinated in limejuice and seasoned with fresh chiles. Limes are also used to season cooked fish, and as juice and garnish for various beverages.

Oranges

Two general varieties of oranges are used in Central America as well. Bitter orange, or Seville oranges (*Citrus aurantium*) are used much like limes as an acid in marinades and sauces especially for meat dishes. Sweet oranges (*Citrus sinensis*) are primarily eaten fresh, out-of-hand. In the home, oranges are commonly peeled, segmented, and used in salads, desserts, and as garnishes on cakes, meats, and poultry dishes. Despite these other uses, it is the juice that makes this fruit so popular in Central America.

Coconuts (Cocos nucifera)

Authorities dispute the origins of the coconut domestication, some placing it in Southeast Asia, others claiming it originates in northwestern South America. Regardless of its origin, the coconut is now found across the tropics. As the familiar fruit is buoyant, it likely traversed significant distances by marine currents, with or without human company. Many communities along the Caribbean coast of Central America, especially Kuna, Miskito, and Garifuna peoples, rely on coconut palms for food, fuel, building materials, and other household needs. For many decades, coconuts have been produced on commercial plantations throughout Central America, mainly for the oil used in the manufacture of soaps and perfumes. In recent times, however, coconut production, yield, and rates of consumption in much of the region (excepting Guatemala and Nicaragua) have declined as a result in large part to coconut tree diseases including lethal yellowing disease and porroca.

Coconuts grow on palms that reach up to 100 feet high and produce clusters of fruits near the top that vary in shape from globular to oblong. The coconut shell is a nearly quarter-inch thick, woody container encased in a thick, fibrous husk that must be cut away to expose the fruit. The edible, oily flesh or kernel adheres to the inside of the shell. A hollow center contains a liquid known colloquially as coconut water or coconut juice. This refreshing sweet beverage is consumed from unripe (green) coconuts. Coconut plays an important role in the cuisine of the Garifuna people who inhabit the coasts of Belize, Guatemala, and Honduras. Coconut oil is used in frying and baking and coconut milk is commonly used in sauces, soups, and one of the signature foods of the Caribbean coast, *pan de coco* or coconut bread.

Pan de Coco (Coconut Bread)

2 pkgs. active dry yeast

2 tsp sugar

1/2 cup warm water

6 cups flour

1/2 cup shortening

13 oz canned coconut milk (or 2 cups fresh coconut milk)

1 tsp salt

2 Tbs. pure coconut oil (can be rendered from fresh or canned coconut milk)

This recipe takes about two hours total time and makes approximately two dozen dinner rolls. Mix together yeast, sugar, and water and let sit covered for 10–15 minutes until bubbly. In a large bowl mix most of flour (5 cups) and salt. Make a depression in the center and pour in the yeast mixture and shortening. Mix with hands. Add coconut milk and mix. Add more flour if the mixture sticks to your fingers. Remove to a floured countertop or other flat surface and knead gently 3–4 minutes; add coconut oil and then knead another 4–7 minutes until smooth. Cover and let rest about 40 minutes in a warm spot or until it doubles in size. Divide the dough into hand-sized balls. Refine shape into rounds and place onto a cookie sheet. Let rise another 45 minutes and then bake at 375°F for 20–25 minutes. They are ready when tops are browned.

Mango (Mangifera indica)

Although native to India and the forests of Southeast Asia, the mango arrived in the tropical Americas during the 16th century and is now well adapted and widely dispersed. Several varieties are used interchangeably for fresh fruit and prepared desserts in Central America. The mango tree is an erect, nearly evergreen tree, 30 to 100 feet high. One, two, or more fruits grow suspended from the branches on short stems and do not ripen until they drop. The fruit is an elongated sphere, slightly flattened and pointed on one end (the beak). Mangos range in size from 8 to 24 ounces depending on variety. The skin is leathery, smooth, and varies in color from light green or yellow with flecks of brown to deep green varieties with blushes of red and purple. The skin is inedible and contains a sap that is irritating to some people. The fruit is eaten at all stages of ripeness, even when green and hard. As the flesh ripens, it becomes a soft yellow, some varieties deepening to a beautiful orange. The texture of a ripe mango is juicy, buttery, and soft, much like a blend of melon and peach. The quality of the fruit depends on the scarcity of fiber and lack of turpentine taste. Mangos are a popular street food, served whole, sliced, or on a stick, and are available throughout the rainy season from the end of May through October.

Melons (Cucumis melo)

Originating in the circum-Mediterranean region, melons are rounded or elongated fruits with skins that range from creamy white to green. They have an edible, juicy pulp, ranging from white, to salmon, to bright red. The fruit is rich in vitamins A and C and is served in salads, ices, preserves, and juices.

Pomegranate (Punica granatum)

Produced from the pomegranate tree, these small fruits have reddish pulp and range in flavor from very sweet to tart. The fruits are ripe when they have developed a distinctive color and make a metallic sound when tapped. The fruits must be picked before overmaturity when they tend to crack open, particularly when rained on. The fruit is eaten fresh or reduced to syrup, known popularly as grenadine, and served over crushed ice.

Tamarind (Tamarindus indica)

Native to tropical Africa, tamarind means the "date of India." The fruit is a beanlike, irregularly curved, and bulged pod. The pods are cinnamon-brown or grayish-brown externally. As they mature, the pods fill out somewhat and contain a sticky, brownish-orange pulp enclosing 1 to 10 shiny black seeds. It is the pulp that is used as a flavoring for its sweet, sour, fruity aroma and taste. There are many food uses of the tamarind. The fully ripe, fresh fruit is eaten out of hand and the pulp is made into a variety of products. Sugared tamarind pulp is often prepared as a confection. Tamarind-flavored beverages, *refrescos*, are made throughout homes in Central America, and they are also bottled commercially with carbonation in Guatemala and elsewhere. Commercial plantations of tamarind trees are found in Belize, Guatemala, and other Central American countries.

Watermelon (Citrullus lanatus)

Watermelon refers to both the fruit and plant of a vinelike (climber and trailer) herb originally from southern Africa and one of the most common types of melons in Central America. Known as *sandia* in Spanish, fresh watermelon is one of the most popular fruits in the region. The related cucumber is also widely consumed fresh in salads and soups. Watermelon is eaten in a variety of ways and is also used to make summer drinks and smoothies. Watermelon contains about 6 percent sugar by weight, the rest being mostly water. As with many other fruits, it is a source of vitamin C.

HERBS, SPICES, AND FLAVORINGS

The regimen of herbs spices and flavors are subject to metatezation more so than any other food items in Central American food culture. In table-top *molcajetes*, cooks meld together Old World stalwarts like garlic, cilantro, and citrus with New World flavors such as chiles, epazote, allspice, annatto, and vanilla.

Some preparations known as *recados* and *sofritos* are key contributors to the complex flavors of Central American recipes. A *recado* is a spicy paste used to season food before and during cooking. There are many different blends including *recado rojo*, a Maya original that usually includes allspice, *achiote*, black pepper, clove, cinnamon, cumin, garlic, oregano, and salt. They key flavor in this *recado* is the juice of sour oranges (Seville oranges), which adds a distinct, acidic fruitiness. A *sofrito*, meaning something fried, is actually a medieval European cooking preparation that came to the New World with the Spanish and Portuguese. It is a mélange of aromatic vegetables, the most important of which are onions, garlic, and cilantro sautéed in lard or oil, the choice of which determines much of the flavor. To this bacon or ham, spices, chiles, and tomatoes, cheese, or coconut milk are added according to availability and regional preferences. A *sofrito* is often prepared as a prelude to rice dishes, soups, stews, and braises, or it may become a sauce in its own right. All of theses mélanges require various base ingredients such as these from the New World.

Native Herbs and Spices

Annatto Seeds (Bixa orellana)

Known also as *achiote*, the seeds are used as a flavoring and food coloring in Central and northern South American foods. For the ancient

Maya, the annatto seeds were an important part of offerings in agricultural rites, and they were also used to dye clothing, bodies, and ceramics. For food purposes, the seeds are usually fried in (animal or vegetable) fat; when the color is released from the seeds they are discarded. The golden-yellow fat is used to fry and add color to vegetables or meat.

Allspice (Pimenta dioica)

Allspice is the dried, unripe berries of a large evergreen tree, native to Central America and the Caribbean. The Spanish explorers optimistically called them *pimienta* because the dried berries look like peppercorns. Over time the name became *pimento* and then "Jamaica pepper" in English, indicating where it is grown. The name allspice, used in North America, was applied to it because it tastes like a mixture of pepper, cloves, cinnamon, and nutmeg. Allspice was used by the ancient Maya and it remains an important ingredient in *recados* today.

Chili Peppers (Capsicum spp)

Peppers have become one of the most important spice ingredients in the world. Recall that the primary purpose of the Columbus voyage was not to discover new lands but to find a less costly route to India, the land of spices. Black pepper, known as *pimienta* in Spanish, was very popular and expensive in Europe during the 15th century. What Columbus found in the New World was a small pungent fruit widely used as a condiment with more potent effect than pimienta. The burning taste in these peppers comes from capsaicin, a substance meant by nature to deter predators; ironically their appeal led to their near global predation by humans. What the New World "Indians" called *aji*, or chiles, came to be known as *pimiento* or masculine pepper. Peppers travel readily and adapt to a wide range of environments. Within the genus *Capsicum* there are five domesticated species and literally hundreds of varieties of peppers including the familiar *jalapeño*, *poblano*, *serrano*, and the milder *anaheim* and bell peppers.

Although peppers are an integral part of Central American food culture, their relatively modest use provides an important point of distinction from Mexican cuisine. The average per capita consumption of chile peppers in Mexico is a staggering 1.2 ounces per day. It tapers off among their neighbors to the South and East. In El Salvador, for instance, the consumption rate is less than 1 ounce per day. For Belize and Guatemala daily consumption is around 0.14 ounces. Chile pepper consumption is negligible in the other four countries of the region.[13]

Aji rojo (red peppers), Panamá. AP Photo/Kathryn Cook.

Chipilín (Crotalaria longirostrata)

A leguminous plant that is high in iron, calcium, and beta carotene, *chipilín* is used as an herb and green vegetable and in soups. In local cuisines leaves of the plant are also used to add flavor and color to the dough for tamales and *pupusas*.

Culantro (Ernygium foetidum)

Culantro is a culinary and medicinal leafy green herb commonly used throughout Central America that is also known as Mexican coriander, long coriander, or *recao*. The herb is mainly used as a seasoning in the preparation of a range of foods including vegetable and meat dishes and sauces. It is sometimes used as a substitute for cilantro but has a much stronger taste and coarser texture. In addition to its culinary usage, *E. foetidum* is commonly used for its well-documented medicinal properties.

Epazote (Chenopodium ambrosioides)

The *epazote* plant is indigenous to Central America and southern Mexico and is used primarily as a leaf vegetable and herb for its pungent flavor.

Historically, it has been cooked with black beans for flavor and its anti-flatulent properties. It is also sometimes used to flavor other dishes.

Hoja Santa (Piper auritu or P. sanctum)

The name means "sacred leaf" in Spanish. The *hoja santa* leaves are large and heart-shaped and have a light, sweet flavor like anise. They are used in soups, sauces, and as a wrapper for tamales.

Loroco (Femaldia pandurata)

Also known as *quilte*, *loroco* is an herb native to Central America. The small green unopened flower buds are used in salads, rice dishes, stews, and sauces. In El Salvador and in Honduras, *loroco* flowers are added to the fillings in *pupusas*.

Mexican Oregano (Lippia graveolens)

Many herbs are called oregano in Central America, but this particular native herb has a stronger and sweeter flavor than the European oregano. Both herbs are used in a similar way, dried and ground into sauces and salads.

Vanilla (Vanilla planifolia)

Vanilla is a flavoring derived from orchids in the genus *Vanilla*. It is native to Mexico but with a long record of pre-Columbian usage across Central America. The Maya used vanilla to flavor their drinks prepared from water, cocoa beans, and spices: The ripe fruit is actually a pod, not a bean, as it is frequently called. Most of the fragrance resides in the seeds and the oily liquid surrounding the seeds. Vanilla is now used primarily in popular desserts including flan, *Arroz con leche*, and *queque de tres leches*

Yucca (Yucca elephantipes)

Not to be confused with the root crop *yuca*, yucca is also known as *itabo*, *izote*, or *daguillo*. The yucca flowers are rich in vitamins (especially thiamine or vitamin B1 and riboflavin or vitamin B2) and minerals (like calcium, phosphorus, and iron). Indigenous people of the Central America eat the flower buds of the various species of yucca that have an acid taste and is slightly spicy. They are now often added to salads or cooked with eggs and potatoes.

Herbs and Spices from Abroad

Bay Leaf (Laurus nobilis L.)

Also known as sweet laurel, bay leaf is used as flavoring and seasoning in soups, meat, stews, fish, sauces, and some desserts. Bay leaves are usually dried and are used whole, crumbled, or ground. As the leaves possess aromatic and stimulant properties, they have applications in traditional medicines as well.

Black Pepper (Piper negril)

One of the oldest and best-known spices in the world, black pepper is indigenous to India. The demand for Indian black pepper had a profound influence on the European economy of the Middle Ages and arguably accounts for the "discovery" of Central America. Today, in Central America black pepper is used primarily as a table condiment but as elsewhere to add flavor to cooked foods of all description.

Cilantro (Coriander satvium)

Cilantro is the pungent leaf of the herb coriander used in Central American cooking, usually as an ingredient in salsas. The term *cilantro* is often used interchangeably with the term *coriander*; however, coriander is technically the dried seed of the plant used as a spice.

Cinnamon (Cinnamonium spp)

The inner bark of a tropical laurel tree cinnamon gains its distinctive flavor from a volatile oil contained in the bark from branches at least two years old. Cinnamon bark known as *canela* in Spanish is widely used as a spice, a condiment, and a flavoring for desserts and beverages including coffee, chocolate, and tea.

Garlic (Allium sativum)

Garlic originates in Central Asia and, like many foods, it traveled to Central America as part of colonial Spanish food culture. Garlic is used in various recipes to add flavor and taste. As with many other flavor enhancers, garlic does double duty as a medicinal plant. Garlic is thought to have therapeutic and antimicrobial properties.

Ginger (Zingiber officinale)

Originating in Asia, ginger is well known as a medicinal plant and since its colonial period introduction to Central America, it has been used to aid digestion, treat stomach upset, arthritis, diarrhea, nausea, common cold, flulike symptoms, headaches, and heart conditions. Ginger is also an important culinary spice and flavoring used in sauces, drinks, and baked goods, especially in Antillean communities along the Caribbean coasts.

Mint (Hierba buena)

Mint is an ancient herb used since antiquity for its culinary, medicinal, and aromatic properties, and all varieties of mint (spearmint, peppermint) used in Central American cooking are known as *hierba buena*. The aromatic flavor of the "good herb" is added to various sauces including *chirmol* and *guacamol,* broth, meats, meatballs, and cooked sauces. Fresh mint leaves are also used as a flavoring and garnish in hot and cold drinks.

Sugarcane (Saccharum officinarum)

Sugarcane originated in New Guinea more than 8,000 years ago. It accompanied human migrations and trade to India and then westward to the Mediterranean, eventually reaching Spain around 715 C.E. Columbus transported sugarcane from the Canary Islands to what is now the Dominican Republic in 1493. The crop was taken to Central and South America from the 1520s onward where sugar largely replaced honey as a sweetener. Sugar is still produced commercially in the region and is an important ingredient in the manufacture of soft drinks and rum, as well as commercial and domestic production of cakes and candies. Sugarcane is also eaten fresh. The stalk is cut into short lengths and the outer peel is removed. It is sliced into strips and chewed to extract the sweet juice.

GRAINS AND NUTS

New World

Amaranth (Amaranthus cruentus)

The pseudo-cereal amaranth originated in Central and South America and was already under cultivation 5,000 years ago. The Inca, Maya, and Aztecs all consumed amaranth as a staple food along with maize and beans. After the arrival of the Spanish conquistador, the cultivation of the crop was banned, as its use in various religious ceremonies posed a threat to missionary priorities. The grains of amaranth are tiny seeds approximately 1/8 to 1/4 inch in diameter. To prepare, they are either boiled or popped like popcorn. The greens of amaranth plant, known as *bledo* in Mexico and Guatemala, are as tasty as, and more nutritious than, spinach and prepared in essentially the same manner.

Ramón (Brosimum alicastrum)

Also known as the breadnut, snakewood or milktree or *iximché*, a name that derives from Mayan language to mean the maize tree. Other common names for *ramón* nuts are *ojoche*, *mojo*, and *mayanut*. Ramón trees were planted in extensive groves by the Maya 2,000 years ago, especially in the Petén region of Guatemala and now tower over the ruins at Tikal where it was a staple in the Maya diet. The small, oval, fleshy, green to green-yellow fruit has yellow-whitish pulp and has a sweet aroma and taste. The seed or nut is boiled and made into a paste or it is roasted then ground into flour or meal. Its dietary importance includes a high protein and caloric content. Breadnut flour is commonly used to prepare tortillas, sweet pastries, or beverages in Guatemala and Belize. The seeds are also used to make a coffee-like drink. The milk-white sap, giving the tree one of its popular names, is also a nutritious drink.

Cashew (Anacardium occidentale)

Known also as the cashew apple or the *marañón* in Spanish, the yellow or red cashew apple is a pseudo-fruit with a strong sweet smell and taste. The pulp of the cashew apple is juicy and is often used as a flavoring for *aguas frescas*. The true fruit is a kidney-shaped drupe that grows at the end of the cashew apple. Contained within the true fruit is the singe seed cashew nut, which is typically consumed as roasted and salted nuts. Cashew nuts are used in confectionary and bakery products. Chopped nuts are used in candies, ice cream cakes, and chocolates.

From Abroad

When the Europeans arrived in Central America, they were eager to reproduce their food culture in the new lands. Wheat (*Triticum* spp) as the source of bread, the veritable "staff of life," was an important source of food security for the transplanted Spaniards. Cultivation of wheat had mixed successes in New Spain. It prospered best in the highlands of Guatemala, Mexico, and parts of Costa Rica, as a result of the similarities in climate to the grain's ancestral Mediterranean homeland. Today most wheat flour is imported and is used mainly to make bread, but also pasta and various bakery products including sweet breads, cakes, and cookies. Today, Central Americans have less than half the per capita wheat consumption of their European or North American counterparts, but imported processed foods made with wheat flour such as breakfast cereals and pastas are now widely available, an influence owing in part to changes in trade and the continued globalization of tastes.

Almonds (Prunus dulcis)

Almonds, too, are indigenous to the Mediterranean and Middle East and as an ingredient, provide an unequivocal Spanish-Mediterranean influence to Central American food culture. They are further significant in that they are wholly imported to the region and add distinctive flavor to sauces, beverages, and desserts.

BEVERAGES

Local Brew

Cacao (Theobroma cacao)

Reminiscent of the tale of snake and apple in Judeo-Christian mythology, an ancient Toltec myth describes Quetzalcoatl, the feathered, serpent god bringing chocolate, to human beings. The popular food of the gods, chocolate caught on with human consumers and is now among the most important and sought-after foods in the world. Despite its popularity as a secular food, chocolate remains an important ingredient in ceremonial beverage in many Central American rites. Among the Ch'orti Indians, direct descendents of the Maya, living in Eastern Guatemala and Western Honduras, ritual beverages like *fresco de cacao*, are prepared with cold water, ground cacao beans, and ground maize are consumed by ritual specialists to help them remain cool during the annual rain-making ceremonies.

Brews from Abroad

Coffee (Coffea arabica)

The tropical countries of Central America provide excellent sites for growing coffee. Although not indigenous to the region, high-quality coffee has been harvested successfully in all countries in the region,

Sorting coffee beans after the harvest, Guatemala. AP Photo/Moises Castillo.

sating from its introduction by colonists in the 19th century. The main type of coffee produced in Central America is the *Arabica* bean (*Coffea arabica*), which is produced in mountainous regions where commercial plantations and small-scale *fincas* can be found. By using different methods of cultivation and post-harvest processing to produce distinct tastes and desired qualities, most of the high-quality beans are exported (a small part is now marketed under fair trade, shade grown, and/or organic conditions). The lower quality beans are often used to produce instant coffee; both products are of great importance to the various national economies of Central America. Not all Central American coffee goes abroad, as it is always possible to find good coffee in the market or restaurants. Coffee is an important social lubricant in Central American food culture and an important vehicle for the expression of hospitality. Visitors in even the most humble homes are typically offered *a cafecito,* "a little coffee," to make them feel welcome. Throughout the region, coffee is served *con leche,* with hot milk and sugar. In Honduras, Guatemala, and Panamá, small amounts of cinnamon or cocoa are sometimes added to coffee as well.

SEAFOOD

Marine fishing is a comparatively minor source of food in Central America. Shrimp and spiny lobster, as well as fin fish and conch are caught in coastal waters, but most of the harvests are exported to the United States. Yet some seafood is consumed in the coastal or insular Garifuna, Creole, and Amerindian communities. Freshwater fish, too, are a source of nutrients for indigenous people. Although it is clear that indigenous populations and their colonizers were fish and seafood eaters, the custom has eroded. Per capita consumption of fish and seafood is low, at about two-thirds the world average. Today people in Central America eat twice as much chicken as they do fish.[14] Explanations for the current low rates of fish consumption include lack of adequate preservation methods and infrastructure, inconsistent supplies, and the high prices of fish compared to most other meat foods. Several types of seafood merit attention as significant elements of Central American food culture.

Corvina (Cynoscion nobilis)

A popular fish, known as the white sea bass in North America, the *corvina* is a fine-textured white fish and can be served broiled, breaded and fried, or sautéed in garlic. Most notably, *corvina* is the preferred fish for *ceviche* a traditional dish of Pacific Coast Central America made of cubed fish, lime or lemon juice, onion, and various spices that include salt and chili. The dish consists of raw seafood, but it is not exactly sushi, as the fish actually cooks in reaction with the citric acid bath of the marinade mixture. Traditionally *ceviche* and related fresh seafood dishes like *tiradito* are spicy, served with diced chiles, and often alongside palate-soothing vegetables such as maize and potato.

Conch (Strombus gigas)

Known as *concha* in Spanish and by various local names including *cambombia* in Panamá, *cambute* in Costa Rica, *caracol abulon* in El Salvador and Guatemala, and *caracol gigante* in Honduras, conch is a large marine mollusk found in the shallow waters near the coasts. It has been an important food source throughout Central America for millennia. Archeological accounts infer its use as a food from the various post-harvest uses of the spiral shells. Artifacts include shells as building material and a durable resource carved into tools, musical instruments, and ceremonial objects. The spiral shell has an iridescent pink nacre (mother of pearl) and is a popular souvenir taken home by tourists. Within the shell is a firm, white, pink-fringed muscle about 2.3 inches in diameter. Conch meat has a mild, sweet flavor; however, it is extremely tough and must be tenderized before cooking. Typically the meat is pounded or marinated in lime juice to tenderize it before cooking.

Grouper (Serrinade spp)

A number of types of grouper are found in Central American waters; all are members of the Serrinade family. Grouper is a favorite fish among cooks because of its sweet taste and availability in markets. It can be prepared easily and in numerous ways, as the flesh is snowy white and can be cut into thin filets or cut thick as steaks. Black grouper and Nassau grouper are among the most desirable followed closely by Red grouper and Warsaw grouper, which are also usually larger and abundant fish.

Snapper (Lutjanid spp)

More than a dozen snapper species (Lutjanid family) are found in the tropical waters around the Gulf of Mexico, including the mutton, vermilion, gray, schoolmaster, mangrove, and yellowtail. All are comparable in taste and texture, but the most popular is the Caribbean red snapper, caught in the Caribbean waters off the coast of Central and South America. The flesh is white, small-flaked, and sweet tasting and is commonly prepared whole and paired with rice and beans.

MEAT AND POULTRY

New World Sources

Only a few animals were domesticated in the pre-Columbian era including the turkey, dog, and honey bee. Meat was a luxury item reserved for the elite or special occasions and much of it was provided through hunting. At the time of contact, the New World was replete with wild game including deer, armadillo, tapir, peccary, and monkeys. Currently the expense of meats such as pork, beef, chicken, and fish also leads some people to seek game-meat to supplement their diets. But centuries of human population growth and related activities have severely diminished Central America's native animal resources. Included among the hunted animals is the nine-banded armadillo (*Dasypus novemcinctus*) known colloquially as *cusuco*, which is especially popular in Salvadoran rural cookery. One of the most abundant big-game animals in Central America is the collared peccary (*Tayassu tajacu*) commonly referred to as *javelina*, a 30 to 60 pound piglike animal. Hunting peccary is legal in some Central American countries, and Costa Rica for instance imposes further regulation through seasonal and bag limits. As with other native creatures, peccaries now contend with the deleterious effects of deforestation and habitat loss.

Another favorite game animal is a large rodent that lives on the grounds of forested areas across Central America. Known as paca in most of its range, but *tepezcuintle* in Guatemala, *conejo pintado* in Panamá, and the *gibnut* in Belize, these critters are considered agricultural pests, as they disturb both root and row, crops but their meat is highly prized. Paca numbers have declined in most areas across their ancestral range from Mexico to Brazil. Several governments have passed laws prohibiting the hunting of *paca* or marketing of their meat. Likewise, the Central American or Baird's tapir (*Tapirus bairdii*), which formerly ranged throughout the region, is under threat. The tapir is a forest-dwelling nocturnal herbivore that forages along riverbanks and forest clearings. Once an important source of meat, the tapir population is now decreasing dramatically as a result of habitat loss and predation. It is officially illegal to hunt tapir, although the laws are difficult to enforce.

Iguana

Current conservation efforts across Central America aim to protect two endangered but traditional game animals: the iguana and the sea turtle. The green and black iguanas (*Iguana iguana*) and (*Ctenosaura similis*) are found throughout the region, and both the lizards and their eggs are sought for food, most often in rural areas where it is also known as the *garrobo* in Spanish or the bamboo chicken or chicken of the trees. Quite unintentionally, iguana gained popularity among Europeans and their descendents during the colonial period when the Catholic Church declared this lizard a type of fish and therefore acceptable for consumption on meatless days. Over the past several decades, populations of wild iguana have been greatly diminished across Central America. Now commercial farms and laws to restrict or forbid hunting aim at regulating supply and satisfying the demand for this favorite festival food. Nicaraguan authorities have instituted a seasonal ban on eating of green iguana in effect from February 1 to April 30, covering Holy Week, during which Nicaraguans traditionally cook dishes made with iguana meat and eggs. The green iguana has a rich flavor because of their diet of leaves and fruits including the papaya, which is said to sweeten and tenderize the meat. One preferred way to eat iguana is grilled and marinated with lime.

Sea Turtles

The leatherback (*Dermochelys coriacea*), loggerhead (*Caretta caretta*), and hawksbill (*Eretmochelysim bricata*) sea turtles were once an important subsistence resource across all of Central America. Historically, coastal inhabitants gathered turtle eggs and hunted sea turtles for their meat. Consumption of turtle meat or eggs was thought to imbue good health, stamina, and virility, and this widely held perception likely contributed to the rapid decline of turtle populations. In a well-known case, the Miskito Indians of Nicaragua, formerly subsistence turtle hunters, entered the turtle-exporting trade in the late 1960s. Turtles had been the cornerstone of their subsistence and social systems. Turtle meat provided the primary source of protein, and cultural norms required that captured turtles should be distributed throughout the local community to honor kinship and other social obligations. Once the Miskito began to hunt and sell turtle for profit, fewer captured turtles were consumed locally; nearly all were sold and shipped away. The Miskito egalitarian ethos emphasizing community-wide sharing and reciprocity broke down, giving way to competitive individualism. With heightened levels of production, the turtle resource collapsed, leaving the Miskito without this important source of food, income, and mechanism for social interaction. In the past several decades, the world's sea turtle population has essentially collapsed. Six of the seven species of sea turtles are endangered or critically endangered, and all face high risk of extinction in the immediate future.

Turtle hunting is now officially illegal in Central America, and various measures including turtle excluder devices for shrimp nets have been required to help protect the turtles. Nevertheless, today some communities retain the right to hunt turtles or gather eggs in their territory for their own consumption and use. Various reports indicate that poached turtles, eggs, and by-kill (accidental) from fishing nets still provide turtle meat for human consumption in many Central American locations. As with iguana, the custom of eating of turtle meat during the Lenten holidays is one of the main threats to turtle survival and population recovery. Turtles occupy one of those ambiguous categories that make it a nonmeat for fasting purposes. Consequently, traditions abound in all of Latin America for eating turtle meat during the Lenten holidays. In an effort to mitigate this behavior, a California-based conservation group wrote the Vatican in 2002, citing in the report that the consumption of turtle meat remains the main barrier to species recovery and asking that turtle flesh be declared a red meat and therefore off-limits to observant Catholics.

Old World Sources

The Spanish brought with them a custom of meat eating that remains popular throughout Central America. Commercial ranching and livestock operations, much like the seafood industry, direct their production efforts toward the lucrative export market. To meet local demand, many people raise free-range animals including chickens, goats, pigs, and some cattle in yards and compounds throughout the region.

Beef

Beef, known simply as carne or *carne de res* in Spanish, is the most expensive and highest status of meats. Thus beef is consumed for special occasions or used more for flavoring than as a centerpiece to meals. When beef is roasted or prepared on the grill, it is known as *carne asada* and is generally preferred well done. The lean, grass-fed beef that comes from Central America is generally tougher than North American cuts. Furthermore, the traditional preservation methods of drying and salting required several steps including soaking, boiling, and shredding to make the meat more palatable, and these methods have been preserved in the recipes of various meat dishes of the food culture.

Indio Viejo

The name means "Old Indian" and may refer to the old tortillas in the recipe. Although the label is not politically sensitive, the recipe is a popular Nicaraguan slow-cooked beef dish with orange and mint. It is served with rice and beans and or fried plantains.

1 lb. flank or skirt steak

2 medium white onions

4 cloves garlic

2 cups orange juice

1 tsp. salt

4–8 tortillas (stale tortillas preferred)

2 Tbs. extra virgin olive oil

1 green bell pepper or other mild pepper

1 fresh orange (Seville sour-orange if possible)

1 small bunch of *hierba buena* (fresh mint)

salt to taste

Chop one of the onions together with two cloves of garlic and add to saucepan with entire flank steak. Add the orange juice and then add water to cover. Bring to a boil for two minutes; cover, reduce heat to simmer until meat is tender (about 1 hour and 40 minutes).

Remove meat, onion, and garlic and reserve the liquid for later use. Separate meat from onion and garlic and set aside to cool. Discard onion and garlic; shred beef into long strips.

Heat the remaining oil in a large frying pan and chop and then sauté other onion over medium heat until soft. Add chopped green pepper and continue to sauté a few minutes more. Mince the two remaining garlic cloves and add them as well.

Tear or crumble tortilla into small pieces. Place in a mixing bowl and combine with 1 cup of the reserved broth; allow mixture to soak until liquid is absorbed.

Macerate the mixture until it forms a smooth paste; stir to remove any lumps. Add it to the paste to frying pan and stir as it thickens to prevent it from sticking to the pan. As the mixture thickens, add the rest of the broth in small amounts to establish a thin-to-medium porridge density. It will take about 15 minutes of constant stirring to cook completely Remove from heat.

Separate mint leaves from stems and chop them very finely. Squeeze the orange for its juice; mix together and stir juice and mint into meal.

Serve and enjoy. *¡Buen provecho!*

Pork

Pigs introduced by the Spanish make for an excellent complement to *mipla*, mixed farming practiced in the New World. Pigs are highly efficient at converting grain and waste foods into meat. Free-ranging pigs forage in the undergrowth or yards and compounds and are then fattened with surplus grain. Pork remains a popular meat, although recent downturns in consumption have been noted. Many Central American dishes feature the loin of pork as well as ham and the skins, which are fried as snack food known as *chicharrones*.

Poultry

Introduced by the Spanish, chickens were readily incorporated into Central American foodways in part because of their similarity to turkeys, making them easy to rear. In Honduras, for instance, chickens and turkeys are sacrificed at Lenca *Compostura* ceremonies for a good harvest. Garifuna people of coastal Central America sacrifice chickens as well as other animals during their *Dugu* ceremonies to honor their ancestors. In both cases, the sacrificed animals are later eaten by participants. In a manner harkening back hundreds, if not thousands, of years, live birds can be bought in the markets of many towns and villages. Likewise, birds can also be purchased fresh or in frozen pieces in the grocery store. As it is

Backyard poultry producer, Guatemala. AP Photo/Jaime Puebla.

comparatively inexpensive, poultry is the clear favorite meat consumed in the region. Annual per capita consumption ranges from 25 pounds in Nicaragua to nearly 66 pounds per person in Belize.[15]

Pollo Encebollado (Chicken in Onions)

1 medium chicken (2–3 pounds) cut into serving pieces

3 Tbs. olive or vegetable oil

3 large white onions thinly sliced

1 cup chicken stock or water

1/2 cup dry white wine

2 bay leaves

Wash chicken and pat dry. Season with salt and pepper. Heat the oil in a large sauté pan or Dutch oven over medium heat. Brown the chicken pieces, a few at a time, on all sides. Remove to a plate, and wick away excess oil.

Add the onions to the same pan and sauté over medium heat until translucent and just beginning to brown. Return the chicken pieces to pan along with the remaining ingredients. Simmer covered 25–35 minutes until the chicken is cooked through and tender. Season to taste, and serve with rice. ¡Buen provecho!

Dairy and Eggs

These ancillary products of imported animal husbandry have further expanded the food culture of Central America. A whole host of dairy products now grace the Central American table. Traditional cheeses known as *queso del pais*, a mild, soft, and salty white cheese, are prepared throughout the region; and many dairy products are salty, as salting was one of the few ways to preserve milk foods during colonial times. Another popular dairy food is *mantequilla blanca* (white butter), also known as *mantequilla crema*, which is a milder form of the sour cream familiar to most North Americans. It is a regular complement to beans and rice in Honduras, El Salvador, and Guatemala. Throughout Central America, whole milk, canned, evaporated, condensed, and ultra high temperature (UHT) milks are available and used regularly in cooking. One of the most important and common uses of milk is in *café con leche*. Eggs, too, are incorporated into many dishes, especially in desserts such as flan, one of the most common desserts in Central America.

Flan (crème caramel)

1 and 1/2 cup sugar

1/4 cup water

4 eggs, beaten

1 can sweetened, condensed milk (14 oz.)

2 cups water

1 cup whole milk

1 tsp. vanilla

1/3 cup sugar

Preheat oven to 355° F. Place 1 cup sugar and water in a heavy-bottomed saucepan and stir to dissolve the sugar. Place over medium heat and boil the sugar, without stirring, until it just starts to turn a honey brown, around 12 minutes.

Remove the caramelized sugar from heat and pour into a 9-inch cake pan or in equal amounts into each of six individual ramekins, swirling to coat the bottom. You may not need all the sugar. Place the cake pan or ramekins in a baking pan large enough to hold them without touching.

In a large bowl, beat together the eggs, condensed milk, whole milk or water, vanilla, and 1/2 cup sugar until smooth. Pour into the cake pan or into each of the ramekins.

Fill the baking pan with enough warm water to come about three-fourths of the way up sides of the containers. Place in the oven and cook until a knife in serted into the center of the custard comes out clean, anywhere from 40 minutes to 1 hour. Do not overcook the flan or it may curdle.

Remove the custard(s) from the water bath and chill well. Run a knife around the edges of the custard; invert over a serving dish and serve. *¡Buen provecho!*

NOTES

1. FAOSTAT, FAO Statistics Division, 2008. Retrieved September 5, 2007, http://faostat.fao.org/site/609/DesktopDefault.aspx?PageID=609#ancor.

2. FAOSTAT Statistics Division, September 5, 2007.

3. FAOSTAT Statistics Division, September 5, 2007.

4. FAOSTAT Statistics Division, September 5, 2007.

5. FAOSTAT Statistics Division, September 5, 2007.

6. B. S., Renvoize, "The Area of Origin of *Manihot esculenta* as a crop Plant: A Review of the Evidence," *Econ Bot* 26 (1972): 352–60; D. J. Rogers, "Studies of *Manihot esculenta* Crantz and Related Species, *Bulletin of the Torrey Botanical Club* 99 (1963): 43–54.

7. David M. Spooner, Karen McLean, Gavin Ramsay, Robbie Waugh, and Glenn J. Bryan, "A Single Domestication for Potato Based on Multi Locus Amplified Fragment Length Polymorphism Genotyping" *Proceedings of the National Academy of Sciences* 102 (2005): 14694–99.

8. FAOSTAT Statistics Division, September 5, 2007.

9. Richard Scaglion, "Kumara in the Ecuadorian Gulf of Guayaquil?" in *The Sweet Potato in Oceania: A Reappraisal*, ed. C. Ballard, P. Brown, R. M. Bourke, and T. Harwood. (New South Wales: University of Sydney Press, 2005).

10. J. Morton, *Fruits of Warm Climates* (Miami, FL: Julia F. Morton, 1987).

11. FAOSTAT Statistics Division, September 5, 2007.

12. FAOSTAT Statistics Division, September 5, 2007.

13. FAOSTAT Statistics Division, September 5, 2007.

14. FAOSTAT Statistics Division, September 5, 2007.

15. FAOSTAT Statistics Division, September 5, 2007.

3

Cooking

As with the array of foods found in Central America, the processes and techniques and materials associated with food preparation also stem from various cultures and places. Some techniques are indistinguishable from those used in North American kitchens; others originate in the cooking traditions of prehistoric Mesoamerica. Likewise, cooking equipment that followed European contact is used alongside indigenous forms, and still others are synthetic adaptations of two or more ideas. Cooking in Central America also defies facile generalization, as the region is itself diverse. Parts are predominantly rural and traditional, where food is prepared over wood fires; other parts are urban and cosmopolitan, where homes are equipped with microwave ovens and the latest kitchen conveniences. Irrespective of the location or circumstances, food preparation the world-over is an activity that is most often performed by women.[1]

Various theories explain this pattern; most posit that food work in particular is compatible with or moreover an extension of childrearing responsibilities. Strong beliefs about gender roles prevail in Central America and widespread cultural norms relegate food preparation to women's domestic role. Across rural Central America, women are involved with multiple phases of the food system, as their duties expand beyond the kitchen to include gathering cooking fuel and water, tending kitchen gardens, tending small stock, and gathering wild foods where available. In urban areas the role may include purchasing foods, and in all places preparing food for family members. In this capacity women also become the important conduits for transmission of cultural information. From their mothers and grandmothers, women pick up zoological and botanical knowledge and learn about food preparation, preservation, and the aesthetics of cuisine along with gaining the many skills and abilities that center on food. The prevailing division of labor is further reflected in separate geographic space.

CULINARY DOMESTIC SPACE

Although Mesoamerica contained many impressive cities at the time of the conquest, most of the area's population was rural and most people were involved daily in growing, processing, and preparing food. The region encompassed thousands of small villages of perhaps 100 people or less that articulated with the great urban centers as vassals of the aristocracy. Archaeologists believe that the houses of the pre-Hispanic agricultural settlements were like those still found in rural parts of Central America— simple, sparsely furnished, and often accommodating multigenerational, extended families. People typically lived in single-room round or rectangular huts made with poles covered by thatch or sometimes grass. In some areas homes were constructed of wattle and daub (a frame of woven twigs plastered with clay) or sun-dried adobe bricks. Roofs were gabled for protection against the heavy seasonal downpours that occur frequently in these latitudes. Each residence usually combined storage and workshop areas where pottery and tools were made. The kitchen, too, would have occupied the only room in the house, where eating was also done and hammocks were slung at night to sleep. Women would cook on a *comal*, a flat griddle for preparing tortilla, or other clay vessel set over a wood fire set in a three-stone hearth on the floor.

Today, kitchens may yet occupy the central room of a house or be detached or semidetached from the main living area after a fashion introduced by the Spanish. A further innovation was the *fogón*, a stove that raises the fire on a mud or stone platform and permits cooking at waist-height. Cooking without electricity is still done on a simple old style *fogón* stove. Foods are cooked in pans on stoves constructed of a mixture of dried mud and sand. Their design is similar throughout the region, but converted 50-gallon oil barrels are also used as stoves. Most stoves are located outside, yet under a roof. Monstrous brick and clay structures are sometimes situated outside in a cooking shed.

Today's cooking implements may include a cast iron *plancha* (cook top) and aluminum pots and pans in addition to the clay. Despite changes in other realms, many people in Central America still rely on wood or other

Mud stove. Courtesy of D. J. Webb.

biomass fuel as an energy source for cooking. More than 50 percent of the households in Nicaragua and Honduras and the World Health Organization report that 1.6 million women and children around the world die each year from respiratory diseases caused by the toxic smoke produced from indoor burning stoves used for cooking.[2] During the last 30 years or more, state government and various nongovernmental organizations have implemented improved stove programs in Central America aimed at promoting greater fuel efficiency, household safety, reduced deforestation, and ultimately reducing indoor air pollution and its attendant health effects.

There is no singular form of a Central American kitchen. Certainly depending on social class and location, kitchens will have an admixture of modern conveniences and traditional equipment. What has remained constant as new consumer goods, including blenders, refrigerators, and the like, are incorporated into food preparation are the sharply divided social roles for men and women. The kitchen remains an important domestic space that allows girls to learn food preparation skills from mothers and older relatives.

FOOD PREPARATION

Although not cooking methods per se, several important, taste-enhancing, predigestive food preparation methods are commonly used in Central American food culture. Among these are soaking, fermentation, and grinding.

Soaking

Soaking is a common and deceptively important technique used for various purposes in the Central American kitchen. Beans are soaked to reduce the cooking time and green plantains are commonly soaked before cooking to enhance flavors or reduce oil uptake. Dried and salted foods including meats, fish, and chiles are also soaked to make them pliable and edible before cooking. Even some earthenware cooking pots are soaked to inhibit cracking during cooking. A common soaking technique known as *desflemar* (meaning literally to blow one's nose) is used to take the strong flavor out of onions or chile peppers or even meat from game animals, by soaking in warm water with salt and lime or vinegar and herbs before cooking or inclusion in fresh dishes.

Nixtamalization is a special soaking technique used to transform maize into *nixtamal* or masa, which is the form of the grain food much of Central America uses in making tortillas, tamales, and various sweet, fried foods. When or where this process originated is not known; however, equipment used in making *nixtamal* was found in an archaeological site in southern Guatemala dating back more than 3,500 years. In *nixtamalization*, dried field maize is first shelled and rinsed. A mixture of water and lime is brought to a boil in a noncorrosive pan. The lime here is not citrus but rather calcium hydroxide or slaked lime, sometimes just called "cal." The loose kernels are cooked in the limewater solution then left to soak for a few hours or overnight. The soaking causes the kernels' indigestible skin, or pericarp, to loosen, slough off, and float to the top. The kernels absorb water and expand three or four times in size, and the lime treatment also imparts high levels of calcium, increases the availability of iron, and liberates vitamin B3, or niacin, for the body's use.[3] An added benefit of the *nixtamalization* process occurs when changes in the pH inhibit microbial activity, creating flour that is less likely to become rancid and with a longer shelf-life than untreated maize flour. Before it can be consumed, the preparation is drained and rinsed several times in fresh water. The swollen kernels, *pozole, posole,* or hominy as it is known in North America, are consumed whole or processed further into masa. Freshly ground masa dough is often available in Central American markets, and many stores also sell masa harina, a dried version of masa that can be rehydrated and used like fresh masa.

Fermentation

Another traditional food preparation technique used in the Central American repertoire is fermentation. Through the seeming magical processes of controlled decay, fermentation preserves and transforms food. Beneficial microscopic organisms are introduced into foods and allowed to remain, grow, and eat the food of interest. Their digestion changes the physical properties of the food, often altering its digestibility, odor, flavor, and nutrient content. Many grains, fruits, and root crops are all fermented in various Central American cuisines. *Pozol*, for instance, is a popular fermented beverage made with *nixtamalized* maize and consumed by Indian and Ladino populations in Guatemala and adjacent parts of southern Mexico. Balls of freshly prepared masa dough are covered with leaves and left to ferment at ambient temperatures for 2 to 7 days. The beverage is prepared by diluting balls of *pozol* in water to produce a thin whitish porridge that is consumed as a basic food in the daily diet. Salt, toasted ground chile pods, sugar, or honey may be added.

Various indigenous groups in Central America produce fermented beverages known as *chichas* made from fruits and other foods. One known as *chicha de yuca* is a beverage made for special occasions among the Pech Indians of Honduras. After it is peeled, the yuca root is boiled then pounded in a mortar. A small quantity is then masticated until it turns into a smooth white quid, which is returned to the mash, diluted with water, covered with *bijao* leaves (*Calathea lutea*), and left to ferment for three days or more while enzymes from the saliva facilitates the fermentation, transforming the entire batch into a mildly alcoholic (2–3%) drink.

For cash crops like cacao and coffee, fermentation is also an important step in processing before marketing. Unlike *chichas*, however, the alcohol produced in this process is a catalyst to change rather than the desired result. When cacao fruits are ripe, the pods are harvested and then usually sliced open by hand to remove the seeds, and the surrounding pulp get scooped out of the pod and dumped into deep wooden boxes to ferment for about a week. The mucilaginous pulp provides the sugar needed for the fermentation process. As the fruit's white flesh decomposes, the outside of the bean contained within starts to oxidize and to turn brown. Simultaneously, the germ within the bean dies from the heat, alcohol, and changed chemical environment. This causes enzymes within the bean to release and break down bitter compounds in the seed, which in turn causes the familiar cocoa aroma to develop. Fermentation also helps remove the tannins present in the cacao bean, which also detracts from the taste of the final chocolate if not removed through proper fermentation. Fermentation times range from five to seven days after which the cacao beans are removed from the sweat boxes and carefully dried before the next steps in refining the commodity.

Grinding

Without question, the significance of maize agriculture was not lost on indigenous people who viewed it as a foundation of humanity and memorialized it in legend lore and plastic art forms.[4] Theirs must have been a love-hate relationship with maize, however, for the rough textured grain that is comparatively easy to grow requires a great amount of effort to transform into familiar and palatable foods. The daily grind was a tedious and laborious process undertaken by women who knelt before one

Metate. Courtesy of D. J. Webb.

Molcajete. Courtesy of D. J. Webb.

or a series of stone *metates*, the three legged concave stone tablet carved from volcanic rock. Using the hand-held stone roller known as a *mano*, women would work for up to five hours a day making the flour needed for the day's meals.

Whereas the *metate* requires horizontal and a full-bodied effort to grind maize, smaller-scale and more delicate grinding tasks were performed with the *molcajetes y tejolates*, or mortars and pestles. Like the *metate*, *molcajetes* were traditionally carved of volcanic rock but differ in that they require a vertical crushing motion and are commonly used in Central American areas adjacent to Mexico for grinding chiles, *pepitas* (pumpkin seeds), cocoa beans, and other spices. The *molcajete* is a vital tool used in the preparation of *pepiáns*, *recados*, and various salsas. It has a simple and elegant form and has enjoyed a recent revitalization among cooks interested in Central American food culture.

Since the 1950s, mechanical devices for grinding have become available to more and more people in the region. Today steel blades and rollers in hand-powered, table-top grinders and even electric food processors or power-driven grain mills have assumed the task of grinding maize and the ingredients for soups and salsas. They have largely displaced the volcanic stone grinding implements from the center of the kitchen to use on special occasions or as decorative objects for display and nostalgia. Technological changes aside, grinding remains an important preparation in many Central American recipes.

COOKING TECHNIQUES

The techniques used in Central American cooking are similar to those known the world over and can be grouped into three basic categories: dry methods, which use hot air or fats to convey heat; wet methods, which use water, other liquids, or steam to cook foods; and a third method that combines qualities of both wet and dry approaches.

Dry Heat Methods

Dry heat methods include toasting, which in Central America is done principally on the *comal*. For instance pumpkin seeds, sesame seeds, spices such as cumin, and garlic are all toasted on the *comal* over high heat before being blended with other ingredients in soups and salsas. Chiles and tomatoes are also cooked over a hot dry *comal* to deliberately blister their skins, thereby changing the taste and texture. As there were limited sources of fat, fried foods were not part of preconquest food repertoire, but pan frying and deep frying in lard or vegetable oils are now popular dry heat cooking methods across the region.

Grilling is another dry heat method and probably the most common form of food preparation in pre-Hispanic Central America. Grilling known as *a la parilla* or *asada* is used especially for coking beef or poultry, but also fresh *elotes* (maize on the cob). Foods are arranged on racks (*parilla*) and exposed to the direct radiant heat and smoke from coals of aromatic wood that convey both flavor and an appealing texture to the foods. Grilling is often done on traditional pottery charcoal braziers known as *anafres*. The top portion of the *anafre* is a short pottery basin about four to six inches high and ten inches in diameter, with holes in the bottom. In this receptacle charcoal is burned as a heat source for cooking, which is done on a *parilla* or a *comal*. The pot is supported by a pottery base that is open on the sides to provide updraft for the coals. *Anafres* are now made from steel or aluminum and are often used by street food vendors to prepare their foods for sale. In Honduras, *anafres* also refers to a bean and cheese fondue-like dish that is served with tortilla chips.

Comal. Courtesy of D. J. Webb.

Wet Method

Examples of foods prepared with wet method cooking include the boiled rice and root vegetables and the tamales or *bollos* as they are known in Belize that are wrapped in leaves and steamed.

Combined Methods

More commonly wet and dry cooking methods are combined, as in the preparation of *guisados* (stews), one of the most popular way of cooking in Central America. In these dishes, meats or poultry are fried in oil or sometimes cooked under pressure and then set aside. A sauce is cooked separately and slowly to build complexity, often in a clay *cazuela*. The two elements are joined to simmer together for a designated time before serving. Popular dishes like *pepián* are examples of *guisados*, or stewed dishes

Pibil or *pib* cooking also combines wet and dry methods of cooking. On the Yucatan—much like the backyard barbeque grill of suburban

Drum stove. Courtesy of D. J. Webb.

North American households—men take charge when cooking outdoor meat feasts. Maya men prepare pit ovens by digging an earth oven lining it with stones. A layer of wood is placed on top and set afire. When the stones become red hot, pieces of *pibil* meat, basted with a seasoning paste—*recado rojo* are wrapped in banana leaves and placed in the oven, which is in turn covered with branches and more earth to cook. Food cooked in this manner has religious significance for the Maya as offerings to agricultural deities must be prepared in the earth itself to be considered appropriate and sanctified fare.

COOKING UTENSILS

Biodegradable Materials

Parts of various plants are used in food preparation and consumption. Many articles are carved from mahogany, *ceiba,* and other hardwoods including bowls and a great variety of spoons, ladles, and stirrers. Another source of biodegradable food container is the *morro* or calabash tree (*Crescentia cujete*). The dried gourds from this tree are carved into daily-use bowls, spoons, and small, open cups known as *jicaras* across the region. Highly decorated *jicaras* are also made for the tourist trade or for use in ritual ceremonies.

Even more ephemeral utensils include the leaves used as storage containers and wrappers for cooking various foods. The leaves help hold in moisture, lend flavors the food, and keep foods from burning and falling apart in the fire. The most common type of foods cooked in leaves are fish and especially the tamale, which is masa dough (*nixtamalized* maizemeal) sometimes packed with fillings wrapped and steamed in *hojas de maiz* (corn husk) or some other leaf. In the more tropical areas of Central America, it is more typical for tamales or *nacatamales* to be wrapped in banana leaves or plantain leaves, which contribute their own unique and subtle flavors.

Chaya (*Cnidoscolus chayamansa*) is an indigenous green of Central America similar to spinach that is also used as an edible tamale wrapper in the Central American highlands. Leaves from the *waha* or rattlesnake plant (*Calathea insignis*) are used to wrap *bollos* in Belize and another Calathea plant (*Calathea lutea*), known locally as *bijao*, is used to wrap tamales in Panamá and Costa Rica. Leaves serve other culinary purposes including lining the *pib* cooking pits and various pots. Leaves also function as green plates that can be easily recycled after the meal. Nicaraguan *vigorón*, a dish consisting of boiled *yuca*, *curtido* (spicy shredded cabbage), and pork rinds, for instance, is commonly served on a plantain-leaf plate.

When woven into basketry, leaves are also associated with food preparation in other ways. Various indigenous groups, including the Kuna, Wounaan, and Emberá of Panamá, create highly decorative basketry that is derived from forms with fairly general functions of gathering, storage, or transporting food or any other valuable. Some baskets, however, are designed with particular food preparation tasks in mind such as those used by the Garífuna to detoxify bitter cassava. The bitter varieties of cassava contain cyanide and are quite poisonous when uncooked. An ingenious use of basketry has permitted this root crop to become an important food for people ranging from the Amazon to the Caribbean. A long cylinder of woven bayal (*Desmonucus* spp) leaves called a *ruguma* is filled with the pulp of peeled, washed, and pounded cassava. One end of the basket is hung from a tree branch, and a stick is used to pull the tube tight and squeeze out all the poisonous juice. The pulp is then sifted in another basket called a *híbise* and the residual pieces of yuca in the sifter are then cooked on the grill to make *casabe*, the flat cassava bread.

Earthenware

Earthenware pots, jars, and grills were used in Central America before European contact and have continued to be used long after metal wares and European pottery were diffused in the region. Local terra cotta vessels have been used for various purposes including food storage, preparation, and serving. Local potters using coil or pinch-pot construction make an array of shapes and sizes, many with rounded bottoms, mimicking the shape and function of *jicaras*, nature's model for containers. Still today, many cooks prefer earthenware pots for the earthy flavors they lend to the foods prepared in them, but as they are made of *terra cotta* (cooked earth) they are subject to cracking and must be soaked in water before use.[5] Some cooks also season these vessels before first use. Common earthenware cooking pots include *cazuelas*, *pucheros*, and *comales*. A *cazuela* is a flat-bottomed bowl with flared sides and a handle on either side of the rim. This pot is glazed on the inside (to hold liquids) and left unglazed on the outside and is typically used to cook stews and soups placed directly over a heat source. Care must be taken to ensure that the glaze used on earthenware vessels does not contain lead, as the metal can leach into foods and affect health. The term *puchero* refers both to the stew and the tall earthenware pot in which it is cooked. These pots are deep with straight sides that hold heat and minimize evaporation. Originating in Spain, *puchero* recipes have been *metatezized* by the addition of New World ingredients such as potatoes and squash and vary greatly in their list of ingredients. Finally, *comales* are unglazed flat pottery griddles used to toast tortilla, seeds, and chile peppers. An analogous vessel known as a *budare* or *budari* is used in southern Central America to prepare *casabe* or *yuca* bread.

Metal Cookware

Today there are cast iron, aluminum, and stainless steel equivalents for all vessels and containers formerly made of earth, stone, or plant material mentioned previously. Because of durability, these industrial-age innovations have found their place among the *batterie de cuisine* of Central American households and are put to the same tasks of boiling, stewing, and toasting as their indigenous predecessors. Some common metal cookware includes the *caldero*, which is a heavy cast iron or aluminum stew pot or caldron used for making rice or slow cooking dishes such as *pepiáns*, *guisados*, or *sopas*. Similar to this in form is the *olla*, a tall pot used for boiling vegetables, pastas, soups, or stews whose name is also the generic term for pots or the soups cooked in them such as *olla de carne*. As they function much like the *puchero*, the terms for these pots are often interchanged. Still used for toasting tortilla, the *comal* is today most often a heavy, cast iron round griddle with a handle and a hole in it for hanging.

COOKING AS A CULTURAL RESOURCE

As many tourists, expatriates, and adventurers refer to their eating experiences when relating travel stories, it is not surprising that the culinary tourism sector has grown in a manner similar to the surge experienced by ecotourism and heritage tourism a decade ago. Beyond dining in restaurants, the culinary tourist seeks local and authentic food experiences to better understand the culture in the places visited. A few pioneering cooking schools have emerged to offer short courses, one to five days' duration; they are often taught in English to fill this niche. Foremost among these is the Antigua Cooking School in the colonial city of Antigua, Guatemala, which features a rotating menu of local ingredients and traditional recipes that accommodate modern cooking methods. Consistent with the philosophy of *metatezation*, various cooking schools in Costa Rica, Belize, and Panamá provide training in local as well as international cuisines including Thai, Italian, and French. Both approaches support local food production and consumptions, which contributes ultimately toward a sustainable tourist industry.

NOTES

1. D. Rogers, *The Domestication of Women* (London: Tavistock Publications, 1981).

2. Rogerio Carniero de Miranda, "Taking Women and Forest into Account: Developing a Woodstove for a Healthy and Sustainable Household in Central America." Presented at the Village Power 2000 Conference of The World Bank. PROLENA/Nicaragua.

3. V. Bressani, E. Benavides, Acevedo E., and M. A. Ortiz, "Changes in Selected Nutrient Content and in Protein Quality of Common and Quality Protein Maize During Tortilla Preparation," *Cereal Chemistry* 67, no. 6 (1990): 515–18.

4. P. C. Mangelsdorf, *Corn: Its Origins, Evolution and Improvement* (Cambridge, MA: Belknap Press, 1974).

5. R. E. Reina, and R. M. Hill, II. *The Traditional Pottery of Guatemala* (Austin: University of Texas Press, 1978).

4

Typical Meals and Cuisine by Region

The Isthmus of Central America subsumes a great geographic expanse that is tropical in latitude, with little annual variation in daylight hours, a circadian fact that affects mealtimes and lifestyles in general. Contemporary patterns of consumption have evolved over centuries, and today the general pattern in Central America is three daily meals plus one or more snacks over the course of the day. The notion of a *typical* meal is difficult to describe, however, as much depends on the cultural group, the colonial history, and socioeconomic status of those at the table. Seasonal variations and regional differences also affect the details of the food culture down to determining the preferred bean to serve in the quotidian plate of rice and beans. This chapter reviews the variables that affect the composition of typical meals and surveys some of the favorite foods eaten at different times of the day.

MEALTIMES

Daily mealtimes have held to a similar pattern over the past several centuries in Central America. In the urban areas three meals are eaten following the European fashion and are designated *desayuno, comida,* and *cena* in the Spanish-speaking zones of Central America and breakfast, lunch, and dinner in the English-speaking zones. In rural areas, the meal pattern is more varied; people may eat only two meals a day depending on the work schedule or other variables described herein. There are also

Nicaraguan boys eating. AP Photo/Esteban Felix.

named snack times: the *almuerzo*, taken at mid-morning and the *merienda* or teatime, which occurs in late afternoon. These customs are kept with great variation across the region but bear some further description.

Desayuno and Almuerzo

The common Central American breakfast is usually a light meal eaten early in the morning. In rural areas, the *desayuno* may include tortillas with frijoles, sprinkled with grated cheese accompanied by hot chocolate, tea or *café con leche* (coffee with milk). For the city person, the tortillas may be replaced with fresh *bolillos* (hard-crusted rolls) or toast with marmalade along with the favored hot drinks. A more affluent or leisurely *desayuno* may include fresh fruit or juice, eggs, tortillas, and refried beans (*frijoles volteados*) garnished with grated cheese or cream and a few wedges of fresh avocado. For some people the *desayuno* is insufficient to carry them through the day and another meal, or more accurately a midmorning snack, is taken at about 11:00 A.M. Known as the *almuerzo*, this meal usually consists of a filling dish such as *gallo pinto* (rice and beans); or, as in Guatemala, the midmorning snack may consist solely of a piece of fruit or a long drink of *atole*, a sweetened maize beverage.

Comida

Throughout Central America, the ideal main meal of the day is a late lunch beginning sometime around 2 P.M. and lasting a leisurely two or three hours and often followed by a siesta or rest time. In Central America as elsewhere in the Spanish-speaking world, the custom of long lunches followed by long siesta has been curtailed by the realities of an accelerated pace of modern life. The meal, however truncated, is known as the *comida* in Spanish and lunch or dinner in English. Most people try to take this customarily heavy meal at home with their family. The *comida* may include courses with a *cocido* (stew or soup) served before the main course, which includes cooked rice or pasta, beans, meat, vegetables, tortillas, and fruit-based beverages (*aguas frescas*). When guests are present, this meal may be followed by the *sobremesa*, a customary period of time to linger and talk over coffee or perhaps an after-dinner drink and dessert course.

Merienda and Cena

Some people also have a sweet break in the late afternoon or early evening, as the evening meal is taken so late in the day. Often a social event like the English high tea, the *merienda* is a distinct gastronomic occurrence in Spanish-speaking countries. One fairly common practice in Central America is to serve leftovers from the earlier *comida*, fresh fruit, and sweet rolls or small pastries with coffee or chocolate. In some uses of the term, the *merienda* is the final meal of the day, whereas the term *cena* is used to describe more formal meals shared with friends or family on special occasions. The *cena* or evening meal is eaten very late in the city around 9 P.M. and is generally not a heavy meal. In the rural areas, this would be based on the staples of tortillas and frijoles and may include a *cazuela* of vegetables seasoned with garlic, onions, tomatoes, and chiles. On holidays and celebrations the *cena* becomes the principal meal of the day.

REGIONAL DIFFERENCES

The seven nations of Central America encompass more than 200,000 square miles an area roughly the size of Texas or France. Within the region, chains of rugged mountains bisect the long Pacific and Caribbean coastlines. The Central American interior is a rugged, mountainous area and one of the most active volcanic zones in the Western Hemisphere. Three main temperature zones are discernible: the *tierra caliente*, "hot country," which extends from sea level to an altitude of about 3,000 feet and has an average yearly temperature of around 75°F; the *tierra templada*, "temperate country," which reaches from about 3,000 to 6,500 feet and has a mean annual temperature of 68° to 75°F; and the *tierra fría*, "cold country," which extends about 6,500 to 9,800 feet and has an average yearly temperatures of 53° to 65°F. Variation in ecological characteristics; flora and fauna, rainfall, soil quality, and accessibility affect the capacity to support farming and ultimately the foods available for the typical diet. For the purposes of this chapter, Central America is divided into three discrete zones: the central highlands, the Pacific lowlands, and the Caribbean lowlands. In addition to the physical characteristics, a history of gastronomic encounters with invaders, conquerors, and immigrants of all stripes has contributed, to a greater or lesser extent, to the culinary peculiarities of each zone. To illustrate the regional character of Central American food culture, a menu of representative meals follows the idealized pattern described.

The Highlands

Approximately 30 million people live in the Central American highlands, a region that begins in the northwest of Guatemala with a series of mountain ranges trending east to west. These ranges, many containing active volcanoes, delimit the broad upland plateaus that span much of Honduras, El Salvador, and the northern third of Nicaragua. Two large lakes, Managua and Nicaragua, are situated in a rift valley that divides the northern from the southern sections of the Central American highlands. In pre-Columbian times, highland settlements in El Salvador, Honduras, and Guatemala were part of the broader Mesoamerican or more narrowly the Maya culture region. Life in these places was characterized by intensive maize agriculture, dense populations with advanced material cultures, social hierarchy, and monumental religious centers. Known from the archaeological record, food products from all over the region also converged in key centers likely through trade and tribute payments. But maize, far and above the most important food to the indigenous peoples, is enshrined in the Maya origin mythology and various ritual practices are interwoven with production yet today. Maize is seen as a life-giving element, produced in sacred locations (*milpas*),

Papusas prepared on *plancha*, El Slavador. AP Photo/Luis Romero.

and its cultural centrality greatly influences the food culture of Central America.

Then as now, farming was the predominant way of life in the highlands, although today it is most often export-oriented production of coffee, cacao, other tree crops, and tobacco rather than subsistence crops. Maize and beans still form the staple diet for the majority of the population. In the northern reaches of the highlands, much of this food is purchased from market vendors rather than produced in the family's *milpa*. Before heading out to the fields, farmers in rural Guatemala start the day with a cup of weak and sweetened coffee accompanied by a few tortillas and black beans made the day before. A midmorning snack around 10 A.M. may be *atole*, a sweet maize beverage.

Elsewhere in the northern highlands, another maize-based snack taken during the almuerzo is the *pupusa*, El Salvador's staple and national dish. A *pupusa* is a grilled, white maize-meal cake stuffed with savory cooked pork, beans, cheese, or other fillings. This traditional Salvadoran dish has origins that stretch back centuries evidence for their preparation has been found in archaeological sites at el Ceren.[1] Customarily they are served with an aged pickled cabbage salad (*curtido*) and tomato sauce or salsa, and are traditionally eaten by hand.[2]

Another maize-based food synonymous with the highlands is the *nacatamale*. Popular in Honduras and Nicaragua, the *nacatamale* is the quintessential food for travelers, as it is neatly packaged in a banana leaf wrapper and the leaves act as a preservative and prevent the food from burning when they are reheated on fires.

Nacatamales

Dough Ingredients

5 cups masa (corn flour) mix

1 cup butter

1 medium onion

1 chile pepper

1 garlic clove

1/2 cup orange juice

10 mint leaves

Filling Ingredients

1-1/2 lb bacon (or salt pork or chicken breast)

3/4 cup raw rice

1 Tbs. cider or red wine vinegar

1/2 cup sour orange juice

1 tsp. *achiote* powder (annatto)

15 slices tomatoes

15 slices green pepper

15 slices onion

15 mint leaves

1 garlic clove, cumin, and onion ground to a paste

banana leaves sufficient for 12 or more

Soak the raw rice in water for two hours. Marinate the chicken strips or bacon in a paste of garlic, onion, cumin, achiote, sour orange juice, and vinegar for two hours. Prepare a *sofrito* with pork fat, onions, green peppers, and tomatoes, and add it to the masa. Fry the finely cut onion, garlic, and chili in lard or olive oil and add them to the masa. Mix in orange juice and chopped mint leaves. Make a soft paste of the flour with milk and water. Heat the butter in a pot and add the flour mixture to it. Cook with stirring till a soft ball of dough forms.

Hold banana leaf with tongs and pass quickly across a stove burner on medium heat several times until banana leaf is pliable Arrange two halves of a banana leaf in a T shape then spread 1/4 cup of the dough into three-inch square in center of smooth side of banana leaf.

Place a strip of meat, a teaspoon of rice, a slice each of tomato, onion, and pepper. Fold the banana leaves over the parcel carefully and tie with a string. Line large stockpot with banana leaves. Stack tamales in basket, folded sides down; cover. Adjust heat to maintain gentle boil and steam until cooked tamale easily separates from the banana leaves, adding more water to the pot when necessary. Cool slightly before serving. Unwrap the leaves. ¡buen provecho!

Throughout the northern and western highlands people take the main meal during the early afternoon. The comida may begin with a snack or antihito, such as chuchitos, which are masa dumplings stuffed with meat, or a bowl of cucumber soup. The main course may be pepián, a signature dish of the Guatemalan highlands served with salad and vegetables. Pepián is one of the many recipes based on the Maya recado, pumpkin seeds, tomato, and chiles. The meal includes various vegetables such as potatoes, pumpkins, and chayote and may have beef or chicken, although it is also commonly served without meat, but always with rice and maize tortilla.

Pepián

2 small whole chickens

2 lb. potatoes (cubed)

1 chayote (cubed)

1 zucchini (cubed)

2 cups fresh green beans (cleaned)

2 cups chicken stock

3/4 cup unsalted pepitas (shelled pumpkin seeds)

2 Tbs. sesame seeds

3 Tbs. achiote paste (or seeds or powder)

8 Tbs. vegetable oil

2 serrano or cayenne peppers (stems and seeds removed)

2 red bell peppers, finely chopped

4 tomatoes, peeled and coarsely chopped

2 small onions, coarsely chopped

2 cloves garlic minced

1/4 lb. tomatillos, husked and chopped

small bunch of cilantro, finely chopped

1/2 tsp ground cinnamon

1 Tbs. baking chocolate

1 tsp. black pepper

Cut chicken into equal parts place in pot with chicken stock over medium heat. Cover and simmer for 30 minutes. Remove stock, set aside for later use.

Grind together pumpkin seeds, sesame seeds, in *molcajete* or spice grinder to fine powder. Transfer to mixing bowl.

In 4 Tbs. oil, sauté all peppers, (both) tomatoes, onions, garlic, tomatillos, cilantro, for 3–4 minutes. Transfer mixture to blender or food processor or *metate y mano*. Blend to thick puree; add to mixing bowl containing ground seeds, mix together thoroughly.

Heat remaining oil in skillet. Return pureed mixture to skillet, heat and stir 5–8 minutes, reduce to thick paste.

Add one cup of reserved stock to paste. Add cinnamon, chocolate, *achiote*, and black pepper to make thick sauce.

Return sauce to stockpot covering chicken. Cover and simmer for 20 minutes. Add water as needed to keep liquid consistency.

In separate pot, boil potatoes, zucchini, and chayote for 10 minutes. Add green beans, boil for 8 minutes more or until all vegetables are tender. Drain cooked vegetables, add to chicken and sauce, and mix gently.

Serve *pepián* over white rice. *¡buen provecho!*

The southern range is higher and more massive and extends as plateaus southward down a central spine of Costa Rica, growing steeper and broader until they span Costa Rica at the border of Panamá, descending gradually in elevation through western Panamá and disappearing completely near the Panamá Canal. The southern highlands of Costa Rica and Panamá lie to the south and east of the Mesoamerican area, and the indigenous people are more similar in their life ways to those of the Caribbean and South America. They live in less complex societies and subsisted through foraging and the shifting cultivation of tubers rather than maize. Perhaps more so than the northern part of the range, the southern highlands were affected by the influx of imported foods from Europe. Costa Rica became an independent nation in 1838, and around that time coffee became an all-important export and source of national wealth. Meat, dairy, and bananas became important to the export economy and, when combined with local products, contributed to the local cuisine. Rice has arguably had a greater impact on reshaping the food culture of southern Central America than any other food. Introduced by the Spanish, rice is now consumed as the preferred daily carbohydrate in Costa Rica and Panamá. It is used as an accompaniment to meals and as an ingredient in soups, stews, puddings, and beverages. The breakfast of choice and national dish of Costa Rica, *gallo pinto* or the painted rooster, is a medley of rice and beans often eaten with eggs and garnished on occasion with avocado or chunks of tomato. Rice is also featured in the typical lunch plates such as *arroz con pollo*, or chicken and rice, and the *casado*, which is literally translated as "married man or newlywed." This meal always contains rice and beans and usually some sort of meat and cooked vegetables (*picadillo*). No mid-day meal would be complete without dessert and a popular choice throughout Central America is *arroz con leche* or rice pudding.

Arroz con Leche (Rice Pudding)

3 cups whole milk

1-1/4 cup water

1 cup rice, short or medium grain

2 cinnamon sticks

1/4 tsp. salt

1 14-oz. can sweetened condensed milk

1/2 cup raisins, soaked in warm water to soften (optional)

2 tsp. vanilla

Simmer milk and water in a large pot, over medium-low heat.

Stir in rice, add in cinnamon sticks, and low simmer, uncovered, until rice is softened, about 20–30 minutes. Stir occasionally.

When rice is soft, remove cinnamon sticks and stir in condensed milk, vanilla, salt, and raisins (optional). Return to a simmering heat and cook for an additional 10–15 minutes or until most of the liquid is absorbed and rice has a pudding-like consistency.

Serve hot, topped with a sprinkle of cinnamon or butter or chill in refrigerator for 2 hours and serve cold. *¡buen provecho!*

Pacific Lowlands

The Pacific lowlands of the isthmus constitute a second geographic zone. The Pacific Coast of Central America extends 1,750 miles and includes six of the seven countries in the region. The identifying characteristic of this zone is the extended dry season, which may reach up to eight months in southern Honduras. High temperatures and high rates of evapotranspiration make this a comparatively arid region throughout much of the year. The dry seasons have favored human occupation since prehistoric times, and the Pacific lowlands remain the most heavily populated of the isthmus and the location of most principal cities of the region. Agriculture, too, is concentrated in these same zones where large-scale production of sugar cane, tobacco, cotton, bananas, other fruits, coffee, and cacao occurs.

Many small villages are scattered along the Pacific Coast of Central America, and in them many people are supported solely by harvesting the mollusks, shrimp, and finfish they catch in nearby lagoons and coastal waters. These artisan anglers are generally poor and their living conditions are roughly similar to their compatriots in the highlands. The daily fare usually consists primarily of beans and rice and sometimes fish and shellfishes, eggs, cheese, coffee, and fruits. When the anglers have a little extra money, some chicken or pork may be included, especially for important occasions. Wealthier farmers and ranchers and commercial anglers with seagoing boats also inhabit the coast. These members of the middle and upper classes have much greater access to foods produced in the region and beyond. With their beaches, rivers, and other attractions, the Pacific lowlands are also destinations for tourists and expatriates who ironically have the greatest access to the choice foods produced in the Pacific Coastal lowlands.

Near Quetzaltenango, on the Pacific coast of Guatemala, the day begins with a *desayuno* of fresh fruits including papaya and bananas, sweet bread, and hot chocolate. People in all social classes of Guatemala have for thousands of years consumed hot chocolate. Artifacts recovered from an Early Classic period (460–480 B.C.E.) tomb site at Rio Azul included vessels inscribed with the Mayan glyph for cacao on the outside and the residue of chocolate on the inside.[3] The Maya ground cacao seeds into a paste mixed it with water, masa, chile peppers, vanilla, honey, and other ingredients. Evidently, froth was a much-desired aesthetic quality in a good cup of Maya chocolate. Throughout the region, people still use *mollilos*, or chocolate stirrers, to aerate and cool their chocolate before consuming.

Maya Revival Hot Chocolate

2 cups boiling water

1 chile pepper (serrano or cayenne) cut in half lengthwise, seeds removed

5 cups whole milk

1 vanilla bean, split lengthwise or (1 tsp. vanilla extract)

1 to 2 cinnamon sticks

8 oz. bittersweet baking chocolate

3 Tbs. honey

In saucepan over medium heat, combine milk, vanilla, and cinnamon, stirring occasionally until small bubbles develop. Reduce heat to low before milk boils.

Add chocolate and honey, stirring while chocolate melts and sugar dissolves. Turn off heat; remove vanilla bean and cinnamon stick, and set aside covered.

In a large saucepan over medium-high heat, add chile pepper to boiling water. Cook until liquid is reduced by half.

Remove chili pepper then stir chile-infused water into chocolate over medium heat, tasting as you go to make sure the flavor is not too strong. ¡Buen provecho!

By the time of the mid-morning *almuerzo*, people seek out cooling drinks for refreshment and relief from the heat. At crossroad stops along the coastal highway or on the beaches, vendors sell *agua de pipa* (coconut water). Typically the coconut is cut in front of the customer to ensure its freshness. Other *licuados* (fruit juice-based beverages) include mango, piña, banana, and watermelon.

The Pacific lowlands, like the adjacent highland area, is bisected by the Nicaraguan depression. To the north of Lake Managua, a line of beaches stretches all the way through El Salvador and Guatemala to Chiapas Mexico, interrupted intermittently by small inlets, estuaries, and patches of mangrove. Moving southward from Lake Nicaragua through Costa Rica and Panamá, the Pacific, small peninsulas, gulfs, and bays with beaches, mangroves, and barrier islands punctuate the coastline and provide the sheltered environments suited for fish and shrimp hatcheries and the niches for other marine resources. The people living along the Pacific coast have exploited these resources since prehistoric times and have consumed from them a marinated, raw fish dish, ceviche. Some archaeologists and historians believe ceviche originated in Peru or Ecuador with the Inca who marinated their fish in a mix of peppers and *chicha*, a fermented maize beverage. Other food scholars claim that ceviche has Arabic origins as its pronunciation is similar to *sebech*, which means sour food in the Arabic spoken in the Moorish Mediterranean.[4] Spanish conquerors brought not only citrus trees, fruits, and juices to the New World, but the influence of the Moorish cooks serving on their ships whose traditions included cooking with these fruits. Over time, ceviche has become popular and widely diffused throughout Central America, as *cevicherías* adapt the recipe to local resources to make ceviche from various fin-fish and shellfishes including conch and sea urchins.

Ceviche de Camarones

1-1/2 lb. medium shrimp peeled and deveined

1-1/2 cups finely chopped onion

3/4 cups fresh limejuice

3/4 cup fresh lemon juice

1 cup finely chopped fresh cilantro

1/4 cup olive oil

1/4 cup finely chopped sweet red pepper

1 hot pepper (serrano or scotch bonnet) finely minced

1 cucumber, peeled diced into 1/2-inch pieces

4–6 cherry tomatoes, diced

1 avocado, peeled, seed removed, cut into 1/2-inch chunks

Blanch the shrimp in a pot of boiling salted water for about 1 minute. Drain and immediately cool down in an ice water bath. Set aside.

Soak chopped onion in a large bowl with water and salt for 15 minutes. Rinse under cool water and then drain. Return onion to bowl and add juices, tomato, peppers, shrimp, and oil; cover and chill for 20 minutes or more.

To serve, gently stir in cucumbers, avocado, and cilantro leaves.

Serve with crackers. ¡buen provecho!

The food specialties of the Pacific lowlands are not limited to seafood. A number of dishes reflect local interests and tastes and of course the blended culinary traditions of the Old and New Worlds. In the cattle-producing Guanacaste province of Costa Rica, a rancher may take a *picadillo de papaya verde*, a ground-meat and papaya topping served with flour tortillas and an *ensalada palmito*, (heart of palm salad). Farther down the coast in Panamá, *sancocho* is a favorite recipe for special occasions or the daily *comida*. A *sancocho de gallina*, for instance, is a chicken soup thickened with various root crops and plantains and flavored with cilantro, onions, and peppers. To complete the meal, *sancocho* is served with *arepas*, coconut rice, and the local beer.

The Caribbean Lowlands

The isolated and sparsely populated narrow band of swamps, mangroves, and rainforest lying to the east and north of the highlands and extending to the Caribbean Sea are known as the Caribbean lowlands. Geographically, the region stretches more than 1,500 miles from coastal Belize, across the northern shore of Guatemala and Honduras, and along the eastern shore of Nicaragua and Costa Rica, and ending at the Gulf of Darien in Panamá. Several groups of small islands lie off the Caribbean coast; some, such as the Islas de la Bahía (Bay Islands) in the Gulf of Honduras, are inhabited by people with their own unique blends of culture and culinary practices.

Throughout the Caribbean lowlands, the climate is humid and tropical with little variation in mean temperature, abundant annual precipitation, and a marked summer rainy season. In the preconquest era, the indigenous people of this region had been only loosely connected to the complex population centers of the highlands. With the exception of several trading ports and coastal military installations, the Spanish authorities exerted little control over the region during the colonial period. Likewise when coastal plantation enclaves were established in the subsequent era, they were populated by Creole laborers from the West Indies, who had few linkages to the prevailing society and culture. The sustained isolation of life in the Caribbean lowlands is reflected in a culinary inclination toward the Caribbean and points beyond. Many meals are built on a base of coconut, plantains or green bananas, and various root foods, and many of the recipe names are recorded in proper or corrupted English. The first meal of the day is breakfast in English-speaking Belize. The typical Belizean breakfast includes scrambled eggs with refried red or black beans along with a cup of sweetened tea, chocolate, or weak instant coffee. The preferred bread accompaniment to any breakfast in Belize is the johnny-cake. The johnnycake is a semidry, baked round flour biscuit, usually served with butter or stuffed with ham and/or cheese. A variant known as fry jacks are similar, made from the same batter, but deep-fried, and served dusted with confectioner's sugar, much like a beignet. Weekday breakfasts for middle class and upper class Belizeans might also include fresh fruit such as pineapple or papaya seasoned with lime juice.

Johnnycakes

4 cups sifted white flour

2 tsp baking powder

1-1/2 oz margarine

pinch of salt

water

oil for frying

Sift dry ingredients in mixing bowl. Stir in margarine then add water to make stiff pliable dough. Knead mixture on cutting board then roll out to 1/2-inch thickness. Cut dough into circles, pierce entire surface with fork, and then fry over medium-hot temperature until golden brown. Drain oil on paper towel, serve warm.

In the coastal town of La Ceiba, Honduras, one of the major Caribbean ports on the coast, people take a mid-morning *almuerzo*. Among the popular snack foods are *baleadas*, *tajadas*, and *casamiento*. Most of the larger Honduran towns have *baleadarias*, simple open-air restaurants selling *baleadas*, a thick 6- to 8-inch wheat flour tortilla, all hours of the day. Plain *baleadas* are served with a smear of refried beans and a dried, crumbly fresh cheese. Other times they are served with any one or more of the following ingredients: a *chirmol* sauce, sliced avocados, scrambled eggs, grilled meats, and *crema*, a thin, sweetened sour cream popular throughout Central America. *Tajadas* are green plantains sliced on the diagonal about 1/4 inch thick, deep fried, and salted. They are popular well beyond the banana-producing coasts. In Honduras, rice and beans cooked with coconut milk is known as *casamiento* (the married one), which is favored as a side dish to many meals, or it may stand alone as a snack.

The broad expanse of coastland known as La Mosquita, stretches eastward from La Ceiba and changes direction at Puerto Lempira, becoming known as the Mosquito Coast as it follows southward into Nicaragua. The town of Bluefields is the administrative capital of the Region *Autonoma del Atlantic Sur* (RAAS) on the eastern shore of Nicaragua. The region is remote, sparsely populated, and largely undeveloped. Bluefields, named after the Dutch pirate Abraham Blauvelt, was once a rendezvous for pirates. It later became the capital of the British protectorate over the Mosquito Coast and was a veritable crossroads, bringing into close contact Europeans, Amerindians, and Africans. Today Bluefields is a small city with a significant Creole population. The now distant connection to the West Indies still resonates in the local culinary specialties. For instance, the traditional dinner in the city of Bluefields is a slow-simmering, coconut-based stew known as *El Rondón*. Piquant coconut-based soups are found throughout the Caribbean lowlands including such famous varieties as the conch soup of the Bay Islands. A proper *rondón* is prepared with fish, beef, poultry, turtle meat, *gibnut*, wild boar or whatever ingredients the cook can "run down," the English term from which the name is derived. In the Bluefields version of the dish, the meats or fish are boiled with peppers, onions, plantains or bananas, and various root foods.

El Rondón (Run Down)

1 lb. fish, cut into pieces (red snapper, or marlin)

1/2 pound chicken, cut into pieces

1 quart chicken stock

2 8-oz. cans coconut milk

1 pound root vegetables (yam, yucca, dasheen, *quequisque*, taro)

2 green bananas

1 medium onion, cut in big pieces

1 celery stalk cut into 1/2-inch slices

1 bunch thyme leaves

salt and pepper

1 bell pepper (leave whole)

1 small bunch cilantro

Peel the vegetables and bananas; cut into small chunks place in a soup pot with chicken broth; cover and let cook.

Fry the onion, celery, and pepper in a bit of oil. Add the fish and continue to fry for a minute or so. Add the coconut milk, vegetables, banana, and seasonings. When the milk separates (curdles) and the vegetables are tender, remove the pepper and serve with rice. Garnish with chopped fresh cilantro.

The Caribbean lowlands continue southward beyond the Mosquito Coast proper, crossing the border of Nicaragua into Costa Rica where the wide low-lying plains become more narrow and continue down the Caribbean coast to the edge of South America. The city of Limón is the chief port of Costa Rica, with a population of about 100,000 inhabitants. Limón, like other towns along the coast of the Caribbean lowlands, has a predominantly English-Creole-speaking population but a food culture that draws from mestizo and indigenous traditions as well. For instance, Limón has its own share of the ubiquitous *sodas* or *soditas,* usually a combination of a family-run restaurant and convenience store found throughout Costa Rica. At *sodas* in Limón, locals imbibe in *aguas de sapos* (toad water), a beverage whose Spanish name conceals its Caribbean ingredients: water, lemon juice, molasses, and ginger. They also purchase foods like *patacones,* the thin slices of deep-fried and salted plantains (*tajadas*) and the *pati* for the afternoon *merienda.* The *pati* (pattie or patty) is a traditional Caribbean meat-stuffed pastry that is found throughout the Caribbean Diaspora including most port towns along the Caribbean lowlands of Central America.

NOTES

1. David L. Lentz, Marilyn Beaudry-Corbett, Maria Luisa de Aguilar, Maria Luisa Reyna, and Lawrence Kaplan. "Foodstuffs, Forests, Fields and Shelter: A Paleo-Ethno-Botanical Analysis of Vessel Contents from the Ceren Site, El Salvador," in *Latin American Antiquity* 7, no. 3 (1996): 247–62.

2. *Curtido* is a savory slaw made with pickled cabbage, onions, carrots, and sometimes lemon juice.

3. Richard E. W. Adams. "Archaeological Research at the Lowland Maya City of Rio Azul." *Latin American Antiquity* 1, no. 1 (1990): 23–41.

4. Arnold J. Bauer, *Goods, Power, History: Latin America's Material Culture* (Cambridge UK: Cambridge University Press, 2001), p. 101.

5

Eating Out

Eating out in Central America is an old custom, as prepared food has been available in marketplaces since precolonial times. The first stand-alone establishments to provide food and drink for sale were likely the tavernas and *posadas* during the 16th and 17th centuries. As more travelers came to Central America, more establishments opened to provide for them. Small hotels and restaurants serving food to travelers opened in Belize in the 19th century including resorts catering to the early wave of tourists.[1] Eateries of all sorts—cafes, sodas, *fondas*, *comedores* and restaurants—have become more common, especially in urban areas across the region. The custom of eating out is still a novelty or special occasion for many Central Americans and is most often associated with travel and travelers. Vendors and shoppers alike still avail themselves of the foods prepared for consumption in the marketplace where prepared foods are sold amid the piles of fresh produce, pottery, woven wears, and other material goods.

The last several decades have witnessed dramatic increases in the options for eating out. Fast food franchise restaurants, both imported and home grown varieties, have sprung up across Central America. In cities and towns the numbers of street and market vendors have grown to parallel the growth in urban populations. The norm for most people remains to eat at home or in the homes of family and friends; however, the custom of returning home for a large family *comida* followed by a siesta, for instance, is in decline. Shortened lunch hours and other changes in the workplace now compel many urbanites to eat away from home at least once a day. Although this may be simply a coffee and *bollilo* (a large, hard roll or bun) on the way to work or a quick snack taken from a street food vendor or a sit down meal at a restaurant, it is a part of the changing food culture of Central America.

Street Foods

According to the Food and Agriculture Organization (FAO) of the United Nations, 2.5 billion people around the world eat street food every day.[2] Street food refers generally to a wide range of foods and beverages including those that are sold ready to eat or are sometimes prepared to order for the customer. In Central America, the street food sector has grown in stride with the recent waves of rural to urban migration. Resource-poor migrants arriving in big urban cities often rely on the less expensive street foods to meet their dietary needs before they become integrated into social networks. Much like the periodic markets, the street food sector has flourished by linking more established urbanites to the agro-dietary traditions and resources of the surrounding area. Many vendors buy their fresh food locally, thus linking urban consumers through their enterprises directly to small-scale farms and market gardens in the urban peripheries. By preparing local, often time-consuming recipes for office workers, students, and others who are unable to return home for meals during the course of the day, street food vendors help to preserve traditional gastronomy and provide resistance to the homogenizing influences of culinary or dietary fashions.

Street food vendors also provide low-cost alternatives to restaurant foods, and street food vending provides low skill employment for migrants who are unable to secure other forms of work. At the low end of the hierarchy of the street food guild are the mobile *ambulantes*, itinerant hawkers who walk along the streets carrying coolers, baskets, or other containers. Their wares may include prepared items such as tamales, empanadas, or prepackaged food and drink such as *aguas en bolsa* (clear plastic bags of water), potato chips, and the bottled soft drinks known in Guatemala and Nicaragua as frescos (short for *refrescos*). *Ambulantes* will also congregate around bus stops and stations to sell sliced fresh fruit and when eaten Panamanian style is topped with vinegar, salt, and pepper. In Costa Rica, for instance, *ambulantes* board buses at stops to sell bagged snacks of sliced yuca, shredded pork, and lime, to the passengers.

Other mobile street food vendors have wheeled-pushcarts with more elaborate fare. *Raspadas*, known also as a *granizada* in Guatemala, is a

Street food *ambulante* in Nicaragua. AP Photo/Mario Lopez.

shaved ice beverage, flavored with syrup of various fruits such as tamarind, mango, and pineapple that is often sold from cart vendors. In Belize, street vendors sell a special beverage made from seaweed or sea moss, well known in the wider Caribbean. The beverage is made by boiling the seaweed for about an hour in water. Milk, cinnamon, sugar and cream, and a flavoring, such as vanilla or strawberry, may be added; spices like nutmeg and on occasion rum are added. It is usually served chilled, is very thick, and is sometimes claimed to have aphrodisiac qualities.

Other vendors including the *heladeros* (ice cream vendors) use carts with bells to announce their arrival in parks or marketplaces. Some fruit vendors have apple corers/peelers mounted on their carts and with theatrical and mechanical flare, they prepare the fruit in plain view of the purchaser as way to ensure the freshness and quality of the purchase.

Street food is also sold in more permanent kiosks or stalls usually located in key locations such as the *Zonas Vivas* found in Guatemala City, Guatemala, or San Pedro Sula in Honduras or the *Zona Rosa* in San Salvador, El Salvador. These hot spots are situated near nightlife activities, transportation centers market places, theaters, churches, parks, and in and around commercial buildings. Kiosks serve food at counters, under a roof, and sometimes providing low-cost seating facilities for diners. The distinction between these food stands and less formal restaurants is not sharply defined. In them, one can purchase hot foods, prepared or semi-prepared in the vendor's home, or prepared to order on grills fueled by coals or portable gas tanks. Fire-roasted *elotes asados* (corn on the cob) are the favored street food in Nicaragua. An important distinction is made between *maíz*, which is dried and mature, and *elotes*, which are fresh corn, in season from about August through October. The *elote asado* is served on a stick for easy consumption, and seasoned with a smear of butter or mayonnaise, and then a topping of salt, limejuice, or chile powder.

Plantains are another staple of Nicaraguan cuisine and the most common way to prepare them on the street is deep fried and served alongside empanadas a fried flour pastry, filled with cheese meats or vegetables. One of the most popular street food snacks in El Salvador is the *pupusa*, a white cornmeal cakes stuffed with savory fillings such as cooked pork, seasoned beans, or a mixture of aged and fresh cheese. They are topped with *curtido*, a tangy cabbage slaw spiced with red chiles and vinegar. A similar snack is available in Belize street food stands known as a *panade*. Street foods vendors in Honduras serve up *baleadas* and *pinchos*, a generic name for grilled meats of any animal origin.

Street food stalls vary in shape, size, construction materials, and their access to amenities including electric power and water. Street food quality also varies and long lines usually indicate higher quality street food vendors. Economic success in this sector depends on reputation and word of mouth advertising, as the street food industry is essentially unregulated. Governments generally lack the personnel and resources needed to monitor and regulate street food enterprises and vendors themselves nimbly navigate the regulations on public vending. Street foods are often prepared in unhygienic ways and then held at ambient temperatures for hours, which permits rapid bacterial multiplication. Other problems associated with food and beverages from street vendors include using unsafe ice to chill beverages and selling homemade frozen drinks. Street food and beverage vendors were implicated in the cholera epidemics that swept through Central America in the 1990s.[3] There are now efforts, including those by nongovernmental organizations and grassroots organization of vendors, to ensure both safe foods for consumers and better quality of life for street food vendors.

Marketplace Foods

Local open air markets, known variously in Spanish as *ferias*, *plazas*, or *mercados*, are found in settlements of all sizes and situated on or near important roads or highways. Larger cities may have more than one market, with each specializing in different commodities or serving different

communities in the city. Markets are classified by their frequency of occurrence and include daily markets and periodic markets, which occur less
frequently, that is, weekly, monthly and so on.[4] The network of periodic
markets found throughout Central America has for centuries brought
rural products to the urban centers where people could purchase foods
for their regular cooking needs. Periodic markets also offer prepared foods
and some food stalls that can qualify as restaurants. At the end of the
1980s, supermarkets served only a tiny niche of wealthy consumers in
the capital cities. By 2003, there were supermarkets in essentially every
provincial capital in Central America. Recent research surveys tally some
600 supermarkets today in the five country study area—Costa Rica, El
Salvador, Guatemala, Honduras, and Nicaragua—and indicate that supermarkets have now captured 36 percent of the domestic food markets.[5]
Central American specialty grocery stores have also become common in
the cities and towns of North America where large numbers of Central
Americans reside. These stores provide a culinary link to the homeland
for expatriates living abroad but serve other functions associated with the
traditional marketplace.

Notwithstanding the recent competition from supermarkets, the daily
and periodic marketplaces remain colorful, vivid, and exciting places that
draw sellers from all over the country and points beyond. Local buyers and
tourists alike select from staple foods as well as specialty items unavail-
able at other markets including especially the herbs and preparations used
for medicinal and religious purposes. In addition to distributing food, the
periodic market plays important social functions by providing places for
securing employment, pursuing courtships, and visiting with family members and friends who have moved away. Periodic market gatherings facili-
tate the spread of news and gossip across disparate networks. Markets are
immensely popular with tourists as well. Chichicastenango, Guatemala is
by far the most famous market in Central America and has operated as
such since the area was first settled by the Cakchiquel Maya in 1200 C.E.
Vendors at the Thursday and Sunday markets in *Chichi*, as the locals refer
to the town and marketplace, sell souvenirs and prepared foods amid the
stalls of colorful stacks of carved wood masks, fabrics, tomatoes, peppers,
and fresh fruits.

In Tegucigalpa, Honduras, there are two open air markets, the San
Isidro market and the Mercado Mayoreo. In Leon, Nicaragua, locals and
tourists alike purchase special marketplace breakfasts of plantains stuffed
with scrambled eggs and cheese. In the central market of San Jose, Costa
Rica, baskets, flowers, hammocks, and souvenirs are sold amid the spices,
meats, vegetables, and fresh seafood booths.

FAST FOODS

Neoliberal economic reforms that began in the 1980s encouraged the entrance of franchised fast food restaurants from North America into the Central American market, changing not only diet but models of business operation in the region. Like grocery stores, fast food restaurants have experienced mercurial growth. Kentucky Fried Chicken (KFC), McDonalds, Burger King, Subway, Domino's Pizza, and Pizza Hut are all commonplace in Central America as are other chain restaurants. The appeal of fast food is the same in Central Americans as in other parts of the globe. The restaurants are usually indoors with air conditioning and bright décor, and they are typically less expensive than a table service restaurant. Like street food they accommodate busy work schedules and the foods themselves carry a certain prestige value. The influx has certainly contributed to change toward dining habits more characteristic of North America as Central Americans become more accustomed to eating on the run instead of lingering over protracted family meals. Similarly, pizza, hamburgers, and frozen yogurt are becoming more common in the diets of Central Americans.

With a nod of their own toward *metatezation*, some fast food restaurants, notably McDonalds, have adapted their menu to accommodate local language, tastes, and food preferences. For instance, *yuca* fries are served in the El Salvador restaurants, and *gallo pinto* appears alongside scrambled eggs and pancakes on the breakfast menu in Costa Rica. In Panamanian and Costa Rican McDonald's restaurants, the featured sandwich has undergone a name change. The large, salted beef patty served with cheese, lettuce, and tomato is known as the "McNifica."

Although international fast food restaurants have found success by accommodating local foodways, home-grown competitors have adopted the quick service restaurant model and realized great regional success, too. Panamá has its own popular fried chicken restaurant known as Pio Pio (the sound a chicken makes in Spanish). The most successful Central American fast food restaurant, however, is Pollo Campero. Founded in Guatemala with a single store in 1971, the chain now has 73 outlets in Guatemala and more than 100 throughout the rest of Central America, Mexico, and Ecuador.[6] The door that opened to introduce fast food franchises to the region swings both ways. To serve the considerable Central American Diaspora in the United States, Pollo Campero has opened many franchises in California and more stores in Houston, Chicago, the Washington, D.C. area, Boynton Beach, Florida, and Long Island. The outlets are located in neighborhoods where significant members of immigrants from Central America reside and have been successful by providing the familiar tastes of home.

Restaurants

The term *restaurant* carries a particular meaning in Central America, referring usually to an upscale dinner place with table service. Restaurants as such are beyond the means of most families. The first restaurants were located in capital cities and presented typically European cuisine to elites in government and industry. Along with cafes, and bars, these establishments were run by Europeans and helped to sustain *Criollo* illusions of the European ideal. The Central American capital cities have become more cosmopolitan, and expatriates foster the presence of restaurants from all parts of the world. In Belize, ethnic restaurants include a Lebanese restaurant in Belize City and Sri Lankan and Indian restaurants in San Ignacio. Some ethnic restaurants cater almost exclusively to the expatriate communities; other foreign eateries, including Chinese, Spanish, Italian, and South American restaurants, appeal to the tastes of middle and upper

Pollo Campero, Guatemala. AP Photo/Javier Galeano.

class families. In Belize and Honduras there are also restaurants serving Garifuna-style foods. With the growth of the tourist industry over the past few decades, restaurants in resort hotels cater especially to tourists' imagined cuisines of Central America. Their menus include fresh seafood and an array of fresh fruits. To accommodate growing interests in culinary tourism, some resorts offer cooking courses or demonstrations to their guests as well.

As with fast foods, franchise restaurants from North America have become part of the food culture of Central America. Fixtures of the suburban United States such as Applebees, TGI Fridays, Benihanas Japanese Steakhouse, and the Outback Steakhouse have brought the custom of casual dining to Central America. Perhaps intentionally, this development has diminished the social distance for North American travelers who may find the familiar places reassuring when visiting the region.

Throughout Central America, a more accessible category of eateries is available for local consumers. Known as sodas in Costa Rica and elsewhere as *comedores* or *restaurantes tipicos*, these small restaurants are often family owned and may be run alongside a *tienda* or *pulperias*, small corner stores. In the countryside these restaurants are found along the roadways

Depiction of informal restaurant, Island Mom's. Courtesy of D. J. Webb.

and were established primarily to serve hearty, inexpensive meals to truck drivers. In the cities and towns, they provide lunch to the working people as well. They often have a single fixed menu, handwritten on a chalk board. The food may also be displayed in buffets or a server will come to the table and take the order. They generally offer similar and limited menus, always rice and beans; the *plato típico* ("typical plate" or dish of the day) usually consists of eggs, beans, sausage, and tortilla in the morning and beef, pork, or chicken with beans, rice, and tortilla in the afternoon or at night. Unless it is a fiesta, people do not eat out a lot and places close relatively early, around 9 P.M. Only in the cities, and mostly on weekends, will restaurants be full and stay open late.

NOTES

1. Richard Wilk. Home Cooking in the Global Village. Caribbean from Buccaneers to Ecotourists (New York: Berg Publishers, 2006), p. 177.

2. Food and Agricultural Organization of the United Nations, February 2007. Spotlight: School Children, Street Food and Micronutrient Deficiencies in Tanzania. FAO. Retrieved February 20, 2008, http://www.fao.org/AG/magazine/0702sp1.htm.

3. J. P. Guthman, "Epidemic Cholera in Latin America and Routes of Transmission," *Journal of Tropical Medicine and Hygiene* 98, no. 6 (1995): 419–27.

4. R. J. Bromley, and Richard Symanski, "Marketplace Trade in Latin America," *Latin American Research Review* 9, no. 3 (1974): 3–38.

5. Julio A. Berdegué, Fernando Balsevich, Luis Flores, and Thomas Reardon, "The Rise of Supermarkets in Central America: Implications for Private Standards for Quality and Safety of Fresh Fruits and Vegetables," http://www.rimisp.org/getdoc.php?docid=898.

6. David Gonzales, "Guatemala Journal; Fried Chicken Takes Flight, Happily Nesting in the U.S.," *New York Times* September 20, 2002, A4.

6

Special Occasions

Central Americans celebrate a great number of holidays and festivals known collectively as fiestas. Food plays important roles in fiestas. Sometimes it provides only gustatory pleasure; at other times eating is formalized or accompanied by rules or symbolic meaning. Many fiestas are closely tied to religious belief and resonate with influences from the colonial era. Given the long importance of agriculture in Central America, numerous fiestas are tied to important stages of food production. Other fiestas celebrate important events in the lives of individuals including baptisms, birthdays, weddings, and funerals. Others still are civic and secular in nature, celebrating nationality or some other senses of identity. This chapter provides an overview of important fiestas as they occur throughout the year. As Central America subsumes great complexity and cultural variation, fiestas with the most relevant gastronomic characteristics are presented to allow the most comprehensive overview.

FIESTA FOOD

Fiestas may be local, regional, or national in scope and may last only a day or span a week or longer. Many have their origins in religion; others are tied to food production, and still others are patriotic or nationalistic in spirit. Celebration for any purpose disrupts the monotony of everyday life in Central America and is a welcomed occasion for cooks to prepare traditional dishes for friends and family. The foods of fiesta—*tamales, gallos pintos, pibs,* and *carnes asadas*—are in many cases the same as daily fare, save that when prepared for a fiesta, cooks will take more time and care in their preparation and better quality ingredients may be included. More people will likely be involved in food preparation, especially when the meal is intended for a larger than usual group. Some fiestas require extensive organization and preparation throughout the year. The task of food preparation presents latent opportunities to form or reinforce the bonds of kinship or friendship. A great number of festivals are celebrated throughout Central America and although not exhaustive, the description of fiestas here organizes the most significant festivals and illustrates the role of food and food culture play in their proper execution.

RELIGIOUS HOLIDAYS

As most Central Americans profess Catholicism, much of the annual schedule of fiestas is derived from the Roman Catholic liturgical calendar. Most of the celebrations include an infusion of indigenous customs and coincide with festivities of secular interest. Most holidays fall within two ritual cycles; others are discrete annual observances.

EASTER CYCLE

Carnival

This holiday begins five days before Ash Wednesday and is one of the movable feasts, so called as it may occur earlier or later year to year in accordance with the Catholic liturgical calendar. This is very much a food festival in that the term *Carnival,* or *Carne vale,* translates to mean "goodbye to meat" and is the celebration that precedes the austere Lenten period. Carnival also marks the onset of the Easter cycle observed throughout Central America, although the holiday has lost much of its original religious significance. The main events occur usually during February or March, culminating on *Mardi Gras* (fat Tuesday) and typically involve public celebrations, and parades that combine elements of circus and public street party where people often dress up or masquerade during the celebrations. In its original practice, people needed to use up all remaining meat and animal products such as eggs and butter before the fasting season and therefore consumed copious amounts of the typical foods in a veritable food-frenzy.

Carnival in Central America is not distinguished by consumption of particular or symbolic meals or foods; however, food plays an important role in marking the transition from festive Carnival to more somber Lent. A custom known as *Entierro de la Sardina* or burying the sardine is practiced in Panamá. A mock funeral is held for the sardine where it is buried at the beach to symbolize the end of Carnival and the burial of hedonistic pleasure in preparation for Lent.

Lent or *Cuaresma*

Lent is the traditional period of penitence and abstinence observed by Catholics in the 40 days preceding the Easter celebration. In sharp contrast to the excesses of Carnival, Lent is defined by the *absence* of food. Church laws once forbade consumption of meat, eggs, milk, butter, and cheese during Lent. The devout still abstain from meat on Fridays and eat sparingly or deprive themselves of favored foods during the entire 40-day period to commemorate Jesus's 40 days of privation in the desert. Various and interesting Lenten food traditions have developed on the metaphorical *metate* of Central America. Most notably, chocolate, which diffused to Europe as a part of the Columbian exchange, affected fasting behavior among European clerics and nobles. It became immensely popular; "on the principle that liquids do not break fasts (*liquidum no frangit jejeunum*), chocolate could serve as a nutritional substitute during fasting periods."[1]

Original Lenten rules proscribed "meat" but permitted fish, mollusks, and crab on the grounds that they were "cold blooded." When Spanish missionaries encountered amphibious and thus ambiguous creatures like iguanas, alligators, sea turtles, and curious New World mammals like the capybara, they sent detailed descriptions in their letters back to Madrid and Rome. Their purpose was greater than scientific; they also asked how to classify the animals, specifically to instruct the indigenous people on what could and could not be eaten during Lent. The papal decisions and classification resonate with consequences into the present. For instance *sopa de garrobo* (iguana soup) is so popular in the Lenten diet of Nicaragua that the government has had to impose an annual ban on hunting, and consumption coinciding with the Lenten period. Conservationists also appealed to Pope John Paul II to reclassify sea turtle flesh as meat to alleviate the annual harvesting pressure brought on the endangered species during Lent.

As a rule, meatless dishes are favored during Lent and include the Honduran *capirotadas*, which are fried dumplings made from maize flour and cheese that are eaten alone or added to a vegetable broth and enjoyed as a main meal. A Lenten food in Mexico shares the same name but is actually a dessert more akin to bread pudding. The Lenten menu in all parts of Latin America includes many sweet dishes. Some have become part of the gastronomic legacy of Central America such as *garbanzos en dulce* (sweetened chickpeas) in Guatemala. In fact consumption of sweets in general increases during the cycle of Lent and Easter, and it is possible to buy sweets sold by vendors on the streets and in the atriums of churches.

Torrejas (Central American Version of French Toast)

1 loaf French or Cuban bread (day-old is preferable)

4 eggs, beaten

2 tsp. dry wine

1 can evaporated milk

1 tsp. vanilla extract

1 tsp ground cinnamon

1 cup sugar

2 cups oil for frying (or butter)

Mix eggs, milk, sugar, wine, vanilla, and cinnamon; cut bread in slices less than 1-inch thick. If bread is fresh, toast slightly to firm up surface. Soak bread in the milk mixture. Fry in hot oil until lightly golden.

Serve with sugar syrup or any other type syrup (e.g., maple, fruit syrup).

Semana Santa

Easter is the most important holiday in the Central American calendar. The festivities beginning the week before Easter on Palm Sunday and continuing through Holy Thursday and Good Friday, climaxing on Easter Sunday, are known as *Semana Santa* or Holy Week. This holiday commemorates the last days of Jesus's life, death, and resurrection. Beginning on Palm Sunday, people numbering in the tens of thousands gather to witness processions in which images of saints, the Virgin Mary, or Jesus are carried around the city and through the main square. In many cities and villages alike, streets are carpeted during Easter with petals, pine needles, and variegated leaves in preparation for Jesus's rebirth. Fasting foods associated with the Lenten season continue to be favored during *Semana Santa*. For instance, Creole families in Belize have a fondness for *hicatee* (freshwater turtle) and rice during Holy Week. In Guatemala, those of Maya descent consume a soup made of cabbage and beef known as *tobic*, accompanied by *joch* (a hot drink made of ground maize, barley, cinnamon, and brown sugar) and cooked fresh fruit such as peaches or pears.

CHRISTMAS CYCLE

The Christmas season begins officially on December 8, the day of the Immaculate Conception (*La Inmaculada Concepcion de la Virgen María*). There is a religious ceremony during which pilgrims visit the many sites dedicated to the Virgin Mary. In Nicaragua, the festival known as *La Purisima* is celebrated in a unique manner. The devoted build altars in their homes made with images of the Virgin Mary wrapped in lights, palm leaves, and flowers, similar in form to the *ofrendas* customary in Mexican Day of the Dead celebrations. Family members, friends, and neighbors are invited to pray to the virgin and sing traditional songs or accompany others with whistles, tambourines, and other musical instruments. The host distributes fruits, traditional sweets, caramels, and various drinks.

Las Posadas

The term *posadas* means literally "the inns" or "the shelters" in Spanish but refers also to the religious and social celebration that takes place on each of the nine nights before Christmas (December 16–24). The holiday commemorates Joseph and Mary's journey to Bethlehem and their search for shelter. A reenactment of this difficult journey is celebrated via communal processions that pass through the streets. Children often lead the procession, and participants carry small, lit candles that are placed in colorful paper shades known as *faroles* (lanterns). The pilgrims make stops at three different homes to ask for lodging. By prior arrangement, the fist two reject them by replying with a chant, but the third, who has agreed to host the Posada, offers them lodging. The group sings carols and *villancicos* (village songs), asks for lodging, and are invited in. There is plenty of food and drinks, as well as special treats for the children and neighbors. In Honduras, the celebration typically includes a meal of *nacatamales*, *torrejas*, and fruit punch. During this pre-Christmas period, people also decorate their homes for the season with nativity scenes.

La Nochebuena y la Navidad

Christmas Eve and Christmas Day (December 24 and 25) are widely celebrated in the region. A Christmas Eve dinner for the family is served very late, either before or after the *Misa de Gallo*, the Rooster Mass at midnight, and usually takes place in the household of one of the family members. Bowls of imported fruits—grapes and apples, peaches and pears—grace the table for decoration, and, although there is no prescribed menu for the *Nochebuena* dinner in Central America, tamales are a favorite on many holiday tables. Special tamales stuffed with turkey, prunes, and raisins are favored in Guatemala, for example. Christmas tamales in Costa Rica are stuffed with potato and served alongside roast pork. In Panamá, people celebrate with ham, *arroz con pollo*, prepared with onions, and vegetables and tamales. Christmas Eve dinner in Honduras and Nicaragua features *nacatamales*, pork or chicken tamales wrapped in banana leaves, rather than the maize husk-wrapped tamales. *Relleno*, a chicken stuffed with pork or beef and stewed in a white or black sauce, is a Creole Christmas favorite in Belize. As Belize is a former British colony, many Christmas traditions in the English fashion are continued including serving roast turkey, cranberry sauce, stuffing, and ham for Christmas dinner followed by black cake, known also as Merry Christmas Cake, a pan-Caribbean confection made with dried fruits, nuts, black food coloring, and preserved with rum. The Belizean version of eggnog, *rumpopo*, also is made with rum and served throughout the holiday season. The popular *postres* (desserts) in Spanish-speaking Central America include *torejas*, flan , and a variety of cakes including *pastel tres leches* (three milks cake), all served with coffee.

Boxing Day

Also known as St. Stephen's Day, the day after Christmas is celebrated in Belize as throughout the English-speaking Caribbean. By custom this was the day when gifts (boxes) were given to slaves, servants, and trades people by their patrons and overseers. The day also marks the beginning of *Junkanoo*, a celebration that originated in the era of slavery in the West Indies and named for a Jamaican folk hero, John Canoe. The time spanning the Christmas and New Year holiday was the only free time allowed for the slaves who would be given new provisions and entertain themselves by dancing, eating, and forming bands and dressing up in various costumes. Between December 25 and January 6, the Garifuna people in Belize, Guatemala, and Honduras celebrate *Junkanoo* with dancing, singing, and masquerades that include gender role reversal in the *Wanaragua* festival. People enjoy this festival and procession, eating typical street foods.

New Year's Eve

Many Catholic families celebrate New Year's Eve by attending mass and having a special meal together. Quite often, there are fireworks and late-night celebrations. One culinary tradition on for the holiday, also diffused from Spain, is to eat 12 grapes in the seconds before the stroke of midnight; the grapes symbolize the 12 months in the old year and the year to come. As the grapes are sweet, so will be the new year.

New Year's Day

The new year is usually celebrated in Central America with a family *comida*, late in the afternoon to accommodate the spirited New Year's Eve celebrations from the night before. Customs vary around the region. In Honduras, a special food served for New Year's Day is tamales. In Costa Rica, one custom is to clean the house to ward off bad luck in the coming year. In a custom more typical of South America, children in Panamá burn effigies of Father Time to greet the New Year. Elsewhere, street parties are held with music, dancing, food, and drinks.

Dia de Los Tres Reyes (Three Kings' Day)

In Central America, the feast of the Epiphany is kept with as much solemnity and importance as Christmas itself. The epiphany refers to the revelation experienced by the Magi or the three eastern kings who saw a star on the night Christ was born and followed it to Bethlehem. Known also as Twelfth Night or Three Kings' Day (*el Dia de los Tres Reyes, la Fiesta de Reyes*, or *el Dia de los Reyes Magos*), the holiday is the climax of the Christmas season. According to the Spanish custom, Three Kings' Day is an occasion of gift-giving, and the gifts exchanged symbolize the gifts of gold, frankincense, and myrrh brought by the kings to the newborn Jesus. In anticipation of receiving gifts of their own, children leave their shoes outside the door the night before or prepare a cardboard box cradle for the baby Jesus to lie in, which is placed under their beds. On the next morning, they wake up to find three presents in the box. In recent years, this tradition has waned and children receive their gifts more commonly on Christmas Eve or Christmas Day. A prevalent and sustained culinary custom, however, is the Epiphany cake or *rosca de reyes*, a sweet bread formed in the shape of a wreath and served after a family lunch on the feast day. The cake is decorated with icing or candied fruit but always contains a trinket such as a ceramic or plastic baby figurine in the dough. The person who finds the treasure, known as a *muñeca*, in the piece of cake becomes the king or queen of the feast. In some traditions the lucky one to get the baby Jesus becomes the *padrino* (godparent) of the figurine from the Nativity until the next year. They are expected to prepare an outfit for the baby and to present the statue for baptism at the Catholic Church on the day of La Calenderia (February 2).

King's Cake (*La Rosca de Reyes*)

1/2 Tbs. active dry yeast

2 Tbs. warm water

1/3 cup milk

3 tbsp sugar

1/4 tsp. salt

3 Tbs. unsalted butter

2 to 2-1/2 cups flour

1 egg

2 Tbs. golden raisins

4 Tbs. chopped mixed candied fruit (e.g., figs, oranges, cherries, citrons)

1 Tbs. chopped nuts or blanched almonds

1 Tbs. sugar

1 ceramic baby figurine, or toy, coin, broad bean or almond (varies with traditions)

Egg wash

1 egg, beaten with 1 Tbs. water

Dissolve yeast in warm water. Set aside for 5 minutes.

Heat milk, sugar, salt, and butter to warm (105°–115° F). Combine 1-1/2 cups flour, yeast mixture, milk mixture, and egg. Mix thoroughly. Add enough remaining flour to form a soft dough. Knead on lightly floured surface about 10 minutes. Place in greased bowl, turning to coat top. Cover and let rise in a warm place until doubles in size (about 1 hour). Lightly knead in raisins, candied fruit, and nuts. Place in greased bowl, turning to coat top. Cover and let rise in a warm place until double (again), about 45 minutes.

Punch down dough and insert the baby figurine. Shape a round loaf; make a 4-inch hole in center and push dough into a ring (*rosca*) about 8 inches across. Place on greased baking sheet. Butter the outside of a 3- or 4-inch custard dish and set it in the hole. Let bread rise in warm place for 30 minutes. Make egg wash and brush on loaf. Press remaining whole candied fruits and whole nuts on top. Sprinkle top with sugar.

Día de la Candelaria (Candelmas)

February 2 marks the end of a novena, a devotional period of prayer occurring over nine consecutive days, dedicated to the birth of Jesus and completes the ritual cycle for Christmas. Part of this tradition involves reenacting his presentation at the temple 40 days after his birth. By custom, the nativity scene is taken down and put away until the next year. In Guatemala, people who celebrated Three Kings' Day together are reunited on *Día de la Candelaria* to close the season with prayers, songs, a candlelight procession, dancing, fireworks, and a dinner of tamales, sweet breads, and chocolate.

OTHER ANNUAL RELIGIOUS HOLIDAYS

Saint's Days, Processions, and Pilgrimages

Cities and towns across Central America venerate patron saints in annual festivals that combine devotion and celebration. Typical practices include masses and a procession of the saint's image or icon from one significant location to another. People submit written petitions and give gifts to these saints in exchange for blessings such as healing, a good crop, or even a spouse. Individuals will often vow to sponsor a *patronal* festival when praying for a holy figure to intercede on behalf of a family member or in giving thanks for good fortune resulting from what seems to be divine intervention. Other fiestas are organized by lay religious organizations known as *cofradias*. In both instances, the ritual fiestas allow hosts to use and expand their support network of allies and ritual kinsfolk or *compadrazgo* (godparents), an institution adopted from Spain and 16th-century Catholic Church practices. In Central America, it has evolved into a vehicle of social mobility and system of long-lasting reciprocal obligations from which people draw support for numerous functions including the preparation and purchase of fiesta meals.

By custom and by contrast, the religious activities of Saint's days are accompanied by dances, music, artisan's fairs, and of course feasting and drinking. Special fiestas occur in locations where Jesus or the Virgin has appeared and/or where miracles have occurred. Every region in Central America has one or more of these holy places and close to a thousand such shrines dot the Central American countryside.[2] Each year hundreds of thousands of devoted pilgrims undertake the arduous journey by foot or oxcart to visit important Central American shrines including the *Virgen of Sulepaya* in Honduras, the *Virgen of Los Angeles* in Costa Rica, the Feast of the Savior of the World in El Salvador, and the Feast of the Black Christ of Esquipulas in Guatemala.

Although overtly Catholic, these pilgrimages actually represent an amalgam of religious practices: For instance, the Maya origin myth (*Popul Vuh*) relates the progenitors' journey to Earth from Tulan, the ancient homeland of the forefathers. Much like pilgrimages in other religious traditions, Maya Indians reenacted the mythical journey through sacred travel to ceremonial centers. The Mesoamerican landscape was also punctuated with sacred sites before the conquest, and in an attempt to Christianize former pagans and their practices, evangelizing Spanish missionaries named towns after saints and co-opted the power of the sites by locating on them churches and sacred shrines. Rural residents who had no churches of their own would visit towns and cities for annual *patronal* fiestas, a custom that grew out of their own traditions to become annual pilgrimages attracting tens of thousands of visitors or more. The town of Esquipulas, Guatemala, for instance, is located on the former trade and pilgrimage route that led to the Maya ceremonial city of Copan in Honduras. Named for a Ch'orti' chieftain, Esquipulas was a place of spiritual significance, known for its sulfurous springs, health-giving earth, and Maya shrine, is now probably the most important Catholic shrine in Central America.

Competing accounts describe the origin of the celebration at Esquipulas venerating the image of a crucified Jesus carved in dark wood and known as the Black Christ or *Cristo Negro*. A large church and later a grandiose basilica were constructed to house the statue and its growing following. The miracles attributed to the image account for the staggering numbers of pilgrims who travel throughout Central America to visit year-round, but especially during the weeklong *Fiesta Del Senor de Esquipulas*, which culminates on January 15. Hundreds of thousands who hope to witness a gesture from the icon or to have a wish fulfilled wait in long lines to pay homage to Jesus and to leave their petitions with the statue. Outside the church, the air is decidedly more festive, with people dressed in colorful native costume and eating traditional foods sold by vendors in and around the Basilica. Pilgrims can also purchase small tablets of white clay, embossed with religious symbols and called *panitos del Señor*, or little breads of the Lord. The tablets are blessed and eaten mostly by women to ensure safe pregnancy, but they are taken as a treatment for everything from broken bones to broken relationships. In the Maya classification system, the clay is a cooling substance (see Chapter 7) and thereby alleviates the hot symptoms of pregnancy or other hot conditions.

The popular *Fiesta Del Senor de Esquipulas* has fostered a following in another way. Numerous Black Christ shrines in Honduras, Nicaragua, Costa Rica, and El Salvador attract small numbers of pilgrims, important for those unable to travel to Esquipulas. Panamá, however, has its own and unrelated annual Black Christ Celebration, the *Fiesta del Cristo Negro de Portobelo*, which occurs on October 21. Although this fiesta has its own history and significance for Panamá, it shares many characteristics with the Esquipulas celebration, notably the annual pilgrimage and the syncretic blending of religious observation and civic celebration.

Día(s) de los Muertos or Dia de los Disfuntos (Day of the Dead)

November 1 and 2 correspond with the Catholic feast of All Saints and All Souls days, but the celebration in Central America is known in translation as the Day(s) of the Dead, and it is altogether a different kind of holiday. It incorporates various elements of the ancient Maya culture belief and practice and 16th-century Catholicism. The festival coincides with the maize harvest and Maya festival honoring departed souls, and, despite the Catholic overlay, this holiday retains core indigenous concepts: the cyclical nature of life, the inseparability of life and death, and the belief that people retain their appetites and remain interested and active in the affairs of their living family members after death. Day of the Dead celebrations in Central America generally do not include elaborate *ofrendas* (altars) and are less exuberant over all than the celebration in Mexico; yet it remains an important holiday.

Over the centuries before the conquest, Europeans had developed their own customs of food offerings and feasting with the dead. These found common cause and melded seamlessly with the Mesoamerican practices. The fiesta is today more similar in spirit and practice to the American observance of Memorial Day than to Halloween. The holidays are typically spent with family and sometimes with community members to celebrate and honor ancestors or others deceased. The pervasive custom in the region is to commemorate deceased relatives by visiting the cemetery plot. In Nicaragua, for instance, people go to the cemetery to clean and decorate the graves and in some cases will spend the night alongside their deceased relatives in the graveyard. In Costa Rica, people attend masses and process en masse to graveyards to visit and attend to graves. In Guatemala, common Day of the Dead activities requires migrants to return to their birthplace to decorate the graves of their friends and family with food, drinks, and flowers. Some people have a picnic meal in the cemetery and another custom is the flying of large kites emblazoned with messages that are read by the souls (*animas*) of ancestors as they pass from heaven to earth on their annual visit. Other families set out baskets of cooked food (roasted ears of maize, sweet potatoes, chayote) in the center of their homes for the benefit of the visiting spirits. The belief is that spirits of the dead feast on the aroma or essence of the food, which is later eaten by the living.

Mayan woman visits relative's grave on the Day of the Dead, Guatemala. AP Photo/Moises Castillo.

In this holiday, the manner of food preparation carries symbolic significance, too. In the Maya areas of Guatemala, special tamales, known as *Mukbil Pollo*, include an elaborate stuffing consisting of raisins, capers, and chicken bones to symbolize the deceased. Befitting the occasion, these tamales are prepared in *pibs*, underground ovens, rather than the stovetop method used for daily fare. In Guatemala, people also prepare a sweetened egg-bread, *pan de muertos*, which is very much like one used in northern Spain to decorate graves on *Todos Santos*. Another dish, *fiambre*, an elaborate chilled salad of meat and vegetables, is believed to have originated in the Extremadura region of Spain and is reserved for this special holiday meal.

Fiambre

Vegetables

8 medium beets

4 medium carrots

2 medium white onions

1 small cabbage

1 head cauliflower

4 cucumbers

1 pound raw green beans

4 large radishes

1 bunch asparagus

1 jar stuffed green olives

6 green onions

1 head romaine lettuce

3 fresh jalapeños

Meats, Cheeses, Eggs

1/2 pound cooked ham, 1/2 pound chorizo

1/2 pound cooked sausage (kilbase)

1/2 pound *mortadella* or bologna

1/2 lb. salami

1/2 lb. *chicharrones* (porkskins)

1 lb. cooked shrimp

2 eggs

1 whole cooked chicken

1/2 pound *queso de capas* (or string cheese)

1 can of sardines

1/2 lb. *queso de Zacapa* or other dried cheese

8 oz. chicken broth

Other

12-oz. bottle of apple cider vinegar or red wine vinegar

1 piece of fresh peeled ginger

1 Tbs. of capers

1/4 tsp. star anise

1/4 tsp. black pepper

1/2 Tbs. mustard

1 bundle parsley

1/4 tsp. mustard powder

1/4 tsp. white pepper

4 or 5 bay leaves

2 stems thyme

Preparation (2 days)

Day 1

Wash and slice beets and green beans and parboil boil each separately. Wash and slice carrots, steam lightly, set aside to cool. Cut cabbage into squares.

Mix these ingredients in a glass bowl or casserole dish. Add enough vinegar with 1/2 tsp. sugar to cover vegetables. Cover container and marinate at room temperature overnight.

Day 2

Boil shrimp, set aside to cool. Hard boil eggs, cool and slice. Slice chicken and cooked sausages and other meats to preferred dimensions. Slice and rinse the onions; place in cold water. Chop bay leaves and thyme. Chop the green onions, radishes, and jalapeño chiles. Slice cucumbers. Drain cans of sardines and olives, set aside.

Dressing

Combine 1/2 cup vinegar with capers, anise, white and black pepper, parsley, mustard powder, wedge of lettuce head, green onions, chicken broth, and salt to the blender and blend until liquefied. If needed, add more vinegar.

To Serve

Place bed of remaining lettuce on serving tray; layer meats, seafood, and vegetables then pour blended mixture on it and mix it in carefully.

Garnish with ginger, bay leaves, thyme, eggs, chicarrones, jalapeños, string cheese, and queso seco. *Buen Provecho!*

LIFECYCLE CELEBRATIONS

Several important lifecycle fiestas in Central America divide a person's life into a series of stages, each associated with a different social status and responsibility. Every stage is both a prerequisite for the stages that follow (e.g., one who has not been baptized may not marry) and an occasion to expand the social network. Each ceremony thus marks transition between developmental stages on the path to becoming a respected adult member of the community. Lifecycle celebrations are found to some extent in all societies. The Kuna Indians of Panamá for instance have a puberty rite for girls known as an *inna suit* that includes a ritual cutting of the hair. A young girl's hair cut short conveys a message to all that she is available for marriage.[3] In Central America, a mélange of Iberian and indigenous customs are used like the haircut to mark important life events. One recurring element in all rites of passage is that the transition is made valid by the presence of guests who share food and drink to consecrate the occasion. The choice of food is therefore less important than the act of social communion.

Baptism

Baptism is an important and necessary celebration for children in Central America. After the conquest, the Catholic sacrament superseded various indigenous naming ceremonies, but because of their similarity in form, they continue to alleviate various folk concerns about supernatural creatures, which might carry away an unbaptized child. In accord with both indigenous and European custom of *compadrazgo*, parents choose godparents or *padrinos* for the child. At the moment of baptism, the godparents and natural parents also become each others' *compadres*. Among the Ch'orti' Maya of the highlands, eastern Guatemala, and western Honduras, this moment is consecrated by the ritual exchange and consumption of a hot beverage of chocolate and maize.[4] *Padrinos* accept the responsibility to raise the child in the event the parents cannot and, more immediately, they are responsible for arranging the baptism ceremony, inviting guests and providing the meal that follows. There is no prescribed menu for this fiesta either. The quality and quantity of the food served to guests at the christening fiesta depend largely on the social level and social ambitions of those involved.

Birthdays

In Central America, birthdays are most often celebrated for children with parties and cake and a piñata, a papier-mâché animal or shape that is filled with candy and small toys. As a game, party goers hit the piñata with a stick to break it open in order to get at the treats. For adults and others, birthdays proper have less importance, but they participate in a yearly celebration on the day of the saint for whom they were named. A special birthday party known as a *quinceañera* or *quince* marks a girl's 15th birthday and her passage into adulthood. With roots in the Aztec coming-of-age ceremony, the *quince* is now preserved in middle- or upper-class families across Latin America and the Diaspora. The lavish event resembles a wedding, with ceremonial clothing, a religious ceremony at church, and a reception. Those in attendance include immediate and extended family members, neighbors, and friends and friends of parents, as this event too is important for reinforcing social networks. A dance in which the principal participants parade and perform is followed by toasts and a banquet. Several rites signify the girl's transition to adulthood. In El Salvador, the ceremony is known as *la Fiesta de Rosa* (Rose Party) and the customary meal is turkey or chicken sandwiches filled with carrots, onions, and radishes. Guatemalan *quinceañera* banquets include tamales and chicken or turkey *pepián*, and, of course, cake. As with other lifecycle events, girls acquire *padrinos* for the quince who sponsor various elements of the event. For instance special *padrinos de queque* are in charge of buying the cake, which may be as elaborate as wedding cake with multiple tiers and decorations. Their role at the fiesta includes setting up, cutting, and distributing the cake to all the guests.

Weddings

Weddings are another important lifecycle ritual that most people experience; however, great range exists in their form across Central America. From the least elaborate end of the spectrum are indigenous customs in Panamá. Among the Guyami Indians, no formal wedding ceremony exists, and for the Kuna, the traditional marriage ceremony's only requirement is for the couple to spend a few nights together in a hammock.[5] At the other end of the range are church wedding celebrations that are similar in form and structure to those performed in Europe and North and South America. Church weddings are often prohibitively expensive, and most marriages are not formalized with ceremonies and licenses. Common-law marriage is the more common practice, and some do preserve indigenous customs including prolonged periods of courtship, and the provision of gifts and labor by the man to the young woman's parents.

Among the Sumu and Miskito a bride price gift includes meat food and firewood to demonstrate both subservience and the suitor's ability to provide for his future wife. Among various Maya groups, a choreographed cycle of ritualized negotiation requires the boy's family to present prescribed gifts of food: bread, chocolate, cooked turkeys, and ritual materials to the girl's family. In some communities the custom only requires a groom to ask for marriage with gifts of cacao seeds.[6] If all parties consent to marriage, supervised visitations occur in the girl's home, where the couple is instructed to eat from the same plate and drink from the same cup. They are lectured on proper deportment and, after a designated period of courtship, they may also be married in a religious ceremony.

Among mestizo families, the size and grandeur of wedding fiestas vary with the resources of the bride's family. As with other lifecycle ceremonies, godparents (*madrinas* and *padrinos*) may be involved, serving as sponsors and guiding the couple through their wedding ceremony. Roman Catholic weddings include a mass in which bride and groom receive communion followed by a reception for the guests held either at a private home, hotel, or restaurant where a banquet is served. In Costa Rica a one-plate meal is common fare at wedding tables. The meal features black beans, rice, a meat, and one or more side dishes such as pasta salad, vegetable salad, or roasted plantains. Weddings in Guatemala include *pepián* and tamales and often feature bell-shaped piñatas that are filled with raw beans, rice, and confetti.

The cake is an essential element in all Central American weddings. In Panamá, the traditional wedding cakes are much like those from the West Indies and are made with nuts and dried fruit and soaked in rum. Others may be sponge cake filed with various ingredients and often covered in meringue. The newlyweds cut the cake for all the guests to witness.

Funerals

Mortuary practices and customs provide another glimpse of the multiple and blended cultural practices in Central America. Among the Guaymí (or Ngwabe) of Panamá, a deceased person's grave is marked by the planting of wild ginger and sometimes a small wooden cross. Close relatives of the deceased observe dietary restrictions that prohibit consumption of salt and meat for a month. At the end of the fasting period, eating restrictions are removed, and mourners partake in a meal with meat and take turns eulogizing the deceased.[7] In Nicaragua, Catholic funerary customs include a daylong *vela* (wake), followed by burial and then a novena for the deceased. This nine-day period of mourning recurs across the region and involves daily praying, singing, and eating and may include community members beyond the family.

The Garifuna have several funerary rites, including the *Dubu*, which is a ritual feast similar to a wake, lasting two to four days to appease the spirits soon after someone dies. Similar in name but not purpose is the *Dugu* or Feast the Dead, which is held in an attempt to please the departed spirits who express their unhappiness in the affairs of the living. The *Dugu* feast is given by the extended family and includes the serving of the foods and beverages enjoyed by the ancestors. When the spirits have begun to consume, everyone else is permitted to partake.[8] Consumption, especially of beverages, is considered integral to the success of Maya rituals as well.

Family members and friends of the deceased ritually consume cacao beverages in mortuary ceremonies.[9]

Although mourners may commiserate by sharing food, providing the
dead is equally important in the Maya tradition. The Maya believe the
deceased enter the afterworld through caves and that they require food
and other materials for the voyage. Food is placed in the mouth and included in the grave are tortilla, cacao, and drinking cups to be used along
the way. Improperly provisioned souls pose a haunting threat to the living
relatives. Finally, as noted in the description of the annual Day of the
Dead celebrations, mourners sustain and nourish their relationships with
their deceased loved ones by way of food offerings.

AGRICULTURAL FIESTAS

The production, consumption, and distribution of crops and animals
dominate daily life concerns for many Central Americans, and festivals
mark those important food production phases. Among various indigenous groups in Panamá and Costa Rica, there is a custom of cooperative
labor for which the host or sponsor of the event is obligated to provide a
Chichería or *chicha* (maize beer) drinking party for the participants. Most
agricultural festivals, however, are fixed on the calendar as Catholic
Holy Days and resemble lifecycle ceremonies in their shared concerns
for fertility and growth. Central American agricultural fiestas are influ-
enced by indigenous or imported customs and, in most cases, by both
traditions.

The rainy season in Central America begins in late April or early May,
marking the beginning of the agricultural cycle. The Maya would traditionally clear their *milpas* of dead vegetation in the late spring and hold
ceremonies to bring on the first rains of the year, before planting the all-
important crops of maize and beans. Families would also perform ceremonies in their *milpas* to ask the earth gods to enrich the soil and make the
seed grow. In the Ch'orti' areas, rain-making rituals continue to be practiced. The ceremonies include a ritual meal and a food sacrifice of *black
chilate* (cacao and maize gruel) and a pair of turkeys offered to the rain
gods at a sacred spring.[10] Another beverage, *fresco de cacao*, is consumed
during the Great Inaugural Rain Ceremony by ritual specialists who must
keep their bodies cool to attract the rain (see Chapter 7).[11]

As the precontact Maya venerated religious symbols such as the cross
that were also important in Christianity, Spanish missionaries were from
their view able to successfully supplant the gods of rain with adoration
of the Holy Cross. Celebrated on May 3, *La Fiesta de la Santa Cruz*, or

the Festival of the Holy Cross, is in reality a fusion of the two traditions, which preserves the function of commencing the planting cycle. In current practice, each family decorates its crucifix with fresh flowers, tropical fruits, and other ornaments.

Other annual festivals commemorate the prolonged stages of food production including San Isidro Labrador's Day. The May 15 fiesta honors the patron saint of farmers and farm animals with parades and fairs, and priests bless crops and animals. In Costa Rica, Oxcart Driver's Day (*Dia de los Boyeros*) is held the second Sunday of March in the village of San Antonio de Escazú. Revelers attend a parade of decorated oxcarts, and local priests also bless animals and crops. Most agricultural festivals celebrate the harvests of the many Central American food crops. Belize, for instance, celebrates the harvests of coconuts and cashews. Panamá has the *Feria de las Flores y del Café*, or the Festival of Flowers and Coffee, in January and in the last weekend of August, Honduras hosts the annual Maize Festival (*Fiesta de Maíz*).

NATIONAL FIESTAS

Central Americans gained independence on September 15, 1821, after 300 years of Spanish rule. Guatemala was first to declare its independence but, as communication was poor in that era, the neighboring countries did not hear of the succession for several weeks afterwards. One of the newer traditions of the independence celebrations is the running of the Central American Freedom Torch from Guatemala to Costa Rica to reenact the messenger's trek to bring the news of independence to the other Central American provinces. All five countries, Guatemala, Honduras, El Salvador, Costa Rica, and Nicaragua share the same Independence Day. A result in part of their brief history as a confederation Central American Independence Day fiestas tend to be designed around broader Central American culture rather than discrete nationalist themes. The celebration, which may last up to two weeks, includes parades with fireworks and speeches. The Act of Independence of Central America is read in schools and people usually celebrate with friends and family.

Known formerly as British Honduras, Belize celebrates its own independence day on September 21, commemorating the 1981 independence from the United Kingdom. Finally Panamá celebrates two national sovereignty days: November 28 marks Independence from Spain in 1821 and November 3, Separation Day, marks the 1903 independence from Colombia. There are other nationalist holidays commemorating military victories, great leaders, and benefactors including November 9, Baron Bliss Day in Belize. Important holidays for the Garifuna include the November 19 Settlement Day in Belize and April 12, Garifuna Day in Honduras. These celebrations are headed by the *buyeis* (shamans), who initiate the celebration with a purification rite, which is followed by historical reenactments, dances, songs, and parades. The fiestas culminate in the night with concerts and festivities and traditional Garifuna foods.

Finally, the somewhat conflicted holiday of *Dia de la Raza* or Day of the Race, is celebrated on October 12 in Central America. Known as *Día de la Hispanidad* in Spain and Columbus Day in North America, the holiday celebrates Cristobol Colon's (Christopher Columbus's) "discovery" of the Americas and the European conquest that followed. The name *Día de la Raza* underscores the point that Central Americans are a people with mixed European and indigenous heritage, and the holiday represents this duality. The holiday further commemorates the birth of the mestizo "race" borne out of the conquest. On this day, celebrations such as the Limón Carnival in Costa Rica may be met with protests and demonstrations. People celebrate their mixture of people, races, and cultures with pride and others register their resentment by tearing down statues of Colon.

NOTES

1. Wolfgang Schivelbusch, Tastes of Paradise A Social History of Spices, Stimulants, and Intoxicants (New York: Vintage Books, 1992), p. 87.

2. Mary Lee Nolan, "The European Roots of Latin American Pilgrimage," in *Pilgrimage in Latin America*, ed. by N. Ross Crumrine and Alan Morinis (Westport, CT: Greenwood Press, 1991), pp. 19–52.

3. James Howe, "Marriage and Domestic Organization among the San Blas Cuna," in *The Botany and Natural History of Panamá*, ed. W. G. D'Arcy and Mireya Correa A. (St. Louis: Missouri Botanical Garden, 1985), pp. 317–31.

4. C. Wisdom *The Ch'orti' Indians of Guatemala* (Chicago: University of Chicago Press, 1940).

5. James Howe, 1985, pp. 317–31.

6. Ruth Bunzel, *Chichicastenengo: A Guatemalan Village* (Locust Valley, NY: J. J. Augustin, 1952).

7. Philip Young, *Ngawbe: Tradition and Change Among the Western Guaymí of Panamá*, 7 (Urbana: University of Illinois' Studies in Anthropology, 1971).

8. Nancie L. Gonzalez, Sojourners of the Caribbean: Ethnogenesis and Ethnohistory of the Garifuna (Urbana: University of Illinois Press, 1988).

9. Keith Prufer, and W. Jeffrey Hurst. "Chocolate in the Underworld Space of Death: Cacao Seeds from an Early Classic Mortuary Cave," *Ethnohistory* 54 (2007): 273–94.

10. J. Kufer, N. Grube, and M. Heinrich, "Cacao in Eastern Guatemala: A Sacred Tree with Ecological Significance," *Environment, Development and Sustainability* 8 (2006): 597–608.

11. J. Kufer et al., "Cacao in Eastern Guatemala," 2006.

7

Diet and Health

Central America is a region of great contrast regarding diet and health. The tropical climates with lush verdant growth mask widespread problems of food production, regular food shortages, and dietary deficiencies. The myriad cultural influences have leant shape to indigenous healthcare practices that often operate alongside or blended with Western biomedicine. In terms of national government oversight of diet and health, Costa Rica stands apart from its neighbors. It has been heralded as the "Switzerland of Central America," in part because of the socialized healthcare system, egalitarian ethos, and overall quality of life for its citizens. Costa Rica records life expectancy and infant mortality rates that parallel many European countries.[1] Put another way, Costa Ricans on average earn roughly one-fourth of the average North American wage. Their per capita healthcare expenditures are about one-tenth of that of the United States, and remarkably they have a life expectancy two years longer than that of citizens of the United States.

The miracle of Costa Rica rests in part on a government-sponsored network of hospitals and clinics that operate throughout the country. A national health insurance program provides low cost health services to the Costa Rican populace. Good health comes from good food as well. A productive agricultural sector supplemented by imports ensures a stable food supply that is 30 percent greater than its average daily requirements. Not all Central American states enjoy the same quality of life found in Costa Rica. Neighboring Honduras, El Salvador, Nicaragua, and Guatemala are more similar to the countries of Eastern Europe in many of the significant indicators of health and nutrition.[2] Panamá and Belize have mixed profiles, falling between the two regional extremes of the prevalent indicators. To a greater or lesser degree, all Central American countries confront problems of undernutrition and malnutrition and their attendant effects: infant mortality, maternal mortality, low birth weight, stunting, wasting, and low life expectancy. Central America also joins other developing nations in a paradoxical nutritional transition. Within the span of one generation, obesity has arisen as a dietary health threat equal in severity to hunger and malnutrition. A host of national, regional, and international agencies now devote much greater attention to addressing the illnesses caused by both undernutrition and overnutrition.

FOOD AND TRADITIONAL MEDICINE

Although accepted, regulated, and widely esteemed today, Western biomedicine, based on Enlightenment science and empirical etiology, was late to develop in Central America. The 16th-century conquistadors brought to the New World what was then state-of-the-art, medical practices and theory. Hippocratic medicine, as it is known today, asserts the four physical conditions—hot, cold, wet, and dry—that are associated with the basic worldly elements of earth, air, water, and fire.[3] Interactions between and among the elements create fluids or humors in the body: blood, phlegm, black, and yellow bile. The hot and dry humor is blood; cold and wet produces bile. Depending on their environment, plants, animals, and thus foods have inherent qualities that can heat, cool, wet, or dry the body. Human health rests on an idealized balance among the four humors, and illnesses were classified according to their humoral symptoms. Foods, with their own humoral properties could be used to bring a sick body back into balance; for example, cooling foods would be prescribed for a feverish or hot body.

Upon their arrival, European explorers found robust indigenous systems of healing. The Kuna, Embera, and Wounaan, indigenous communities of Panamá, have complex beliefs about the interconnectedness of human physiology with the natural environment and spiritual realm. In their worldview, medicinal plants and the knowledge to use them are both thought to originate in the supernatural world. Healing acts are equal parts practical acts of medicine, nutrition, and religion. As with so many cultural practices diffused to the New World, Hippocratic medicine blended with and amended these local thoughts and customs. Among the readily shared concepts were the notions of essence and opposition. In the indigenous American cosmology, animate and inanimate objects contain an innate life force or *essence* that affects the essence of others when they are brought into contact.

In the Maya cosmology, essences are organized into patterns of paired opposition with components that complement and complete rather than compete with one another.[4] Male and female, night and day, sky and earth, fire, and water are important couplets; one existing without the other is both unhealthy and ultimately unsustainable. The essences are organized further into complexes of female, night, earth, moon, and water grouped in distinction from male, day, sun, and fire. In this scheme, human beings are part of the cosmological fabric, and much thought and activity go into balancing the influences of these competing moieties to ensure good health and the continuation of the world.

A ready example of this philosophy can be found in food production practices. *Milpas,* or cultivated gardens, are open fields where sun hits the ground and are thus part of the fire, day, and male domain. By contrast, the *monte* or uncultivated forest is cool, damp, shady, and female and must be kept in proportional balance to areas under cultivation to ensure continued health of both elements. Food production activities such as planting or field burning are inherently hot and are scheduled with deference to the essentially cooling influences of the lunar phases.

As with the Hippocratic tradition, food is an important prescriptive and prophylactic vehicle for healthcare throughout Central America. In both traditions, food is organized into conceptual categories of hot and cold that reflect *essential* value more so than thermal properties. For denizens of the New World, food plants such as maize and chile peppers thrive in full sunlight and are therefore considered hot. Plants that grow in wet or shady places, such as beans or cacao, or those that grow underground, such as cassava or especially juicy or sour fruits, would be classified as cool. Their essential properties are transmitted to the consumer through eating, and thus there is a strong prescriptive dietary belief requiring the ingestion of a correct balance of hot and cold foods.

Good health arises from equilibrium between these opposing forces of nature. Breaking the equilibrium between the forces by overindulging in a certain food or neglecting to eat its complementary opposite could result in illness for the individual, the family, or the community, as all are ultimately connected to, and thus affected by, one another. Overbalance in other dimensions of life causes illness as well: excessive work or overexposure to hot or cold weather makes a person sick. Likewise, lack of respect for, or adherence to, customs may also disrupt the balances and cause sickness in the group.

The cosmology and healing practice of the Maya have had great influence on the folk medicine found throughout Central America. African people carried to the New World their knowledge of medicinal plants, which was in turn blended with Spanish, other European, and even Asian beliefs and practices. Much like the *metatezation* of foods, ideas, and practices about healthcare have been melded, adapted, and transmitted from generation to generation in a form of folk medicine with remedies that are often tried and refined at home under the guidance of elders. A popular cure for stomach discomfort likely diffused from Europe is to drink the liquid in which rhubarb or chamomile has been steeped. Self-treatments such as these have the advantage of being immediate and free of charge; however, there are always occasions when further expertise is required.

A full spectrum of highly respected traditional healthcare providers exists in Central America, and most receive spiritual calling to heal and regard healthcare as social responsibility or a "cargo" that must be carried for the good of the family, village, and proper continuation of the world. Important traditional specialists include midwives, bonesetters, massage therapists, people who prepare the dead for burial, and, most important, *curanderos(as)*. All use hot/cold schema in their diagnoses and provides care for the sick at physiological, social, and spiritual dimensions. *Curanderos(as)* use foods in the conduct of their trade more so than other specialists. *Curanderos(as)* or healers are usually older people, long-time residents of their barrio or pueblo and known by word of mouth for their particular healing specialty. Some are asked to help remove negative spirits or the spirits of deceased persons that may be affecting the family's health. More commonly, they are consulted for their diagnostic ability and knowledge of herbs and folk remedies.

A healing treatment may involve several sessions with the *curandero(a)*. In other cases, the client will be sent to herbal pharmacies known as *botánicas* or to market stalls where they purchase a list of herbs and/or materials to be self-administered over a longer period. To restore humoral balance, patients drink *tisanes*, with decidedly hot or cool energies concocted from steeped or boiled herbs, roots, or barks. The use of cacao and chiles, for instance, is well documented as ingestible medicines. Other decoctions are applied externally in the form of poultices or therapeutic bathing.[5] It is a common practice in Belize, for instance, to bathe feverish children in a mango-leaf decoction. Sweat baths are another procedure with multiple origins used for purifying the body and ridding it of unhealthy humors for women after childbirth but also for sick persons with certain fevers, poisonous bites, bee stings, and rheumatism.

Diet

A healthy diet provides the individual with food energy and nutrients required to perform different types of biological work. Because energy needs vary with age, sex, average body size, climate, and physical activity level, establishing a universal recommended caloric intake is a complex approximation fraught with contention. In their approach, the Food and Agriculture Organization (FAO) takes into account the age and sex distribution of each nation's population, the people's average body size, and the country's climate, and then includes a 10 percent buffer for "normal" activity beyond minimum life-sustaining levels to allow for energy needed to undertake physical work and play. In some recent reports, a 3,000 kcal per person per day diet along with varying amounts of water is recommended for an average adult human (about 150 lbs.) to achieve food security.[6]

Current thinking in nutritional science has it that caloric needs are best met by consuming high energy-yielding foods, notably carbohydrates and neutral fats. Ideally, carbohydrates would make up between 55 and 60 percent of the total energy content of the diet, with neutral fats contributing between 25 and 30 percent. Proteins, or more accurately the eight amino acids that comprise the building blocks of protein, contribute 10 to 15 percent of the total caloric content. Proteins are not generally included in the diet for energy, but rather to satisfy the body's needs during growth and development and in periods of high stress including illness, injury repair, gestation, and lactation. An adequate and balanced diet would also provide specific amounts and types of dietary fiber, and as many as three dozen other important vitamins and minerals or micronutrients. As with many other places around the world, Central American diets depart from the outlined ideals in significant ways (Table 7.1).

Nutritional demographers assert that when the average daily food consumption drops below the 2,200 kcal level, it is an indication of undernourishment in the population. Measured in gross caloric values, two Central American countries have dietary levels that are only slightly higher than the figures posted for sub-Saharan Africa. Like that region, Nicaragua and Guatemala have struggled to address chronic and sporadic levels of undernutrition in the population.

Second, the Central American diet is built primarily on vegetal foods (maize, beans, rice, and tubers), which provide on average 82 percent of daily calories, often to the exclusion of other sources of nutrition. For instance, the average annual consumption of meat in Central America was 108 pounds per person in 2003, compared with an average of 271 pounds

TABLE 7.1

Change in Dietary Energy Supply (kcal/person/day) for Central American Countries

Country	1979–81	1989–91	2001–03
Belize	2,770	2,580	2,840
Costa Rica	2,510	2,780	2,850
El Salvador	2,300	2,450	2,560
Guatemala	2,290	2,340	2,210
Honduras	2,120	2,310	2,360
Nicaragua	2,270	2,230	2,290
Panamá	2,270	2,270	2,260

Source: Based on Food and Agriculture Organization of the United Nations (FAO), FAO Statistical Yearbook 2005–2006 Dietary energy, protein, and fat consumption (http://faostat. fao.org), 2007.

per person in the United States.[7] Similar discrepancies exist for the consumption of fats of all origin, dairy foods, and fresh vegetables.

Differences may seem appreciable on the surface, but the Central American diet appears in the long view to be changing in the direction of its North American neighbor, owing in part to the massive rural-urban migration and the increased availability and popularity of prepared or prepackaged foods. Over the past few decades, Central Americans have increased their consumption of wheat products, especially breads, cereals, pastas, and pastries, which are supplanting maize and the traditional foods made from it. Other dietary trends include a marked increase in the consumption of milk and meat products, fruits, and vegetables, as well as fats and sugars. In urban areas, fast foods and prepared foods are more readily available and, in addition to convenience, carry a certain prestige value for the consumer.

The external influence has been less pronounced in rural areas; however, workers returning from stints abroad often bring along their tastes for foods prepared with sugar, refined flour, and animal fats. The noted upward trend in caloric consumption and greater availability of imported foods has done little to affect the pronounced inequality in access to food that exists in the region. Consequently, various forms of malnutrition remain a serious concern throughout Central America.

MALNUTRITION

Malnutrition is a health condition that develops when the body does not get the proper amount of protein, energy, or micronutrients needed to maintain healthy tissues and organ function. The state of malnutrition is often characterized by malaise, susceptibility to infections and disease, and developmental disorders when experienced by children. The term *protein-energy malnutrition* (PEM) is used to describe a broad array of clinical conditions. At one end of the spectrum, severe forms associated with famine, natural disaster, and war include kwashiorkor (characterized by the presence of edema) and nutritional marasmus (characterized by severe wasting), both of which have high fatality rates. Milder expressions of PEM expressed mainly as poor physical growth in children is the most usual form of malnutrition in Central America. Known also as chronic undernutrition, or simply hunger, undernutrition is a consequence of consuming too little energy or using calories more rapidly than they can be replaced. Poverty or lack of monetary income to acquire food is the major problem, but food access is further complicated by social factors such as geographical isolation, ethnic group membership, and household composition characteristics. Undernutrition is affected further by factors such as availability of safe drinking water and sanitation. Water quality greatly affects the incidence of infectious diseases and diarrhea, which may in turn compound ill effects of hunger via rapid weight loss (Table 7.2).

Despite a protracted period of focused developmental effort, no Central American country has seen its absolute number of undernourished decrease, and in Guatemala and Panamá, the proportion of undernour-

TABLE 7.2
Changes in Total Population and Prevalence of Undernourishment in Central America from 1990–1992 and 2000–2002

Country	Total Population in Millions		Proportion of Undernourished in Total Population	
	1990–92	2000–02	1990–92	2000–02
Belize	.26	.3	7	5
Costa Rica	3.2	4.0	6	4
El Salvador	5.2	6.3	12	11
Guatemala	9.0	11.7	16	24
Honduras	5.0	6.6	23	22
Nicaragua	3.9	5.2	30	27
Panamá	2.5	3.0	21	26

Source: Data from FAOSTAT Yearbook 2005; UN Population Prospects Information Division FAO—Food and Agricultural Organization of the United Nations, Viale delle Terme di Caracalla, 00100 Rome, Italy.

TABLE 7.3
Percentage of Undernourished Children (Ages 3–59 Months) Measured by Three
Anthropometric Indices

Country	Year of Survey	% Stunted (height-for-age)	% Wasted (weight-for-height)	% Underweight (weight-for-age)
El Salvador	2002–03	18.9	1.4	10.3
Guatemala	2002	49.3	1.6	22.7
Honduras	2001	32.9	1.0	18.4
Nicaragua	2001	20.2	2.0	9.6

Source: Data drawn from Monteith R. S., P. W. Stupp, and S. D. McCracken. Reproductive, Maternal, and Child health in Central America: Trends and Challenges Facing Women and Children. El Salvador, Guatemala, Honduras, and Nicaragua. Atlanta, GA: Centers for Disease Control and Prevention, 2005.

ished persons increased in the 10-year period ending in 2002. Undernourishment estimates developed by the United Nations' FAO indicate that more than 20 percent of the population suffer from hunger in four Central America countries: Guatemala, Honduras, Panamá, and Nicaragua.[8]

When lean times do occur, children are more prone than other family members to exhibit symptoms of malnutrition. Most nutrition surveys carried out in developing nations concentrate on children under five years old to determine the extent of deficiencies affecting families and communities. When children are undernourished during the most critical years of development, it leads to retarded growth including deficits in height for age (stunting), ill effects that are largely irreversible (Table 7.3).

In Guatemala, nearly half of all children under five years old are chronically undernourished. In El Salvador, Honduras, and Nicaragua, 30 percent of children under the age of five years are affected. Children in poor, indigenous, and rural communities suffer the worst rates of stunting across the region. Growth retardation in children, as measured by weight and height, reflects a combination of various nutritional deficiencies but, in particular, deficits in protein and basic energy. The number of undernourished people had slowly but steadily decreased over many decades, but recent figures presented by FAO illustrate that the number has increased in spite of the commitments to fight hunger.[9]

Recurring Challenges to Food Security

After 30 to 35 years of intermittent political instability and internal military violence, Guatemala, Nicaragua, and El Salvador all emerged in the 21st century with democratically elected governments and two-thirds of Central America's undernourished population. Vagaries in the climate caused by *el Niño*, and *la Niña*, drought, hurricanes, and earthquakes have, over the past decades, exacerbated the situation by substantially reducing food production throughout the region.

At the external level, the region's great reliance on export agriculture has aggravated the situation further. A glut in the world market for coffee and cereal grains for instance caused a serious decline in prices, affecting both family income and food security. The slowing global economy has affected Central American food security in many other ways. Remittances from family members working abroad, for instance, have slowed, and a weakened U.S. dollar means the money sent home from workers in the United States and elsewhere buys less than before. The cost of rice has tripled and beans have doubled over the past year (2008); maize is up 83 percent and wheat is up 70 percent. Predictions on global food prices anticipate an upturn of between 20 and 50 percent by 2016. Price hikes in basic foods hit the urban poor the hardest, as their access to food is precarious, and they are forced to spend a higher percentage of their total income on feeding their families. In various agency publications, the United Nations World Food Program has warned of a looming nutritional crisis in Central America.

Deficiency Conditions

Other pernicious forms of malnutrition, which also affect quality of life in Central America, are the various deficiency conditions arising from the absence of particular vitamins or minerals in the diet. These conditions rarely exist in isolation and are commonly symptoms of more general PEM. Among the more prevalent dietary deficiencies found in Central America is iron deficiency anemia (IDA). The condition arises from an abnormally low concentration of hemoglobin in the red blood cells. The weakened cells are less able to carry oxygen to the tissues, limiting the amount of energy carried and released from the cells, thereby affecting all bodily functions. Roughly one in four children in the region suffers from the condition. Iron deficiency in young children impairs physical growth, cognitive development, and the immune system. During school age, IDA is also associated with impaired motor development, coordination, language development, and overall scholastic achievement.

In adults, IDA causes fatigue and reduced work capacity. IDA increases morbidity from infectious diseases because it adversely affects several immune mechanisms. Throughout the region, a range of mild to moderate levels of anemia occurs among women in the 15–49 age range. Compiled data report occurrence of anemia in 8.5 percent of women in El Salvador, 14.7 percent in Honduras, and 20.2 percent in Guatemala.[10] Prevalence of anemia is attributed primarily to lack of quality foods and blood loss from parasites; however, pregnancy and breastfeeding drain iron stores, making women of reproductive age an especially vulnerable segment of the population. This health problem is addressed by fortifying foods with iron and other nutrients.

Vitamin A

This important nutrient is found in animal foods, especially in the liver and other internal organs. Vitamin A is not usually eaten; rather, it is synthesized in the human body through the consumption of various fruits and vegetables, especially yellow and orange ones with high levels of beta carotene. The prevalence of vitamin A deficiency in children under 5 years old in the rural population ranges from 8.5 percent in Panamá to 22.5 percent in El Salvador.[11] The condition affects many physiological systems including vision and eye health. Night blindness, and xerophthalmia are two common eye conditions resulting from vitamin A deficiency. Other effects include increased maternal mortality rates and other poor outcomes in pregnancy and lactation. Lack of vitamin A may also contribute to higher child mortality rates and affect growth and susceptibility to infection and anemia in children.

Vitamin B_{12}

A high prevalence of low plasma vitamin B_{12} concentrations has been reported in both sexes and across age groups in Central America, particularly among the lower classes, whose diets are often narrowly focused on maize and beans.[12] The deficiency is commonly associated with a diet lacking animal-based foods. Although the condition may be asymptomatic, vitamin B_{12} deficiency can also result in a blood disorder called a megaloblastic or pernicious anemia, which enlarges red blood cells so that the body's own immune system destroys them at an increased rate.

Overnutrition

Paralleling the high levels of undernourishment found in Central America is an opposite ailment, which also affects a surprisingly high number of people. Overnutrition results when a person eats too much food, or too many of the wrong foods. Effects of overnutrition are measured anthropo-

TABLE 7.4
Prevalence of Overweight (BMI ≥ 25 kg/m²) and Obesity (BMI ≥ 30 kg/m²) among Adults
in Central America

Countries	BMI ≥25 (%) Males	BMI ≥30 (%) Males	BMI ≥25 (%) Females	BMI ≥30 (%) Females	Mean Value BMI
Belize	44.7	7.9	54.9	18.6	25.1
Costa Rica	53.9	13.4	57.8	24.2	25.5
El Salvador	43.5	7.4	54.0	17.8	25.0
Guatemala	56.9	15.7	65.4	29.7	26.6
Honduras	37.6	5.2	49.4	14.4	24.5
Nicaragua	52.9	11.5	68.1	34.3	26.6
Panamá	46.5	8.8	56.3	19.8	25.3

Source: Data from Ono T., Guthold R., Strong K. *WHO Global Comparable Estimates,* 2005, http://www.
who.int/infobase IBRef:199999a1.

morphically by way of the body mass index (BMI). A person's body mass
is a single number (index) determined by the weight in pounds divided
by height in inches, multiplied by 703. By convention, a person with a
body mass index higher than 25 is defined as overweight, and one with an
index number greater than 30 is considered obese (Table 7.4).

Throughout the region, the incidence of overweight and obesity is most
common among women, with levels now ranging near or above 50 percent in all seven countries. Guatemalan women have the highest prevalence of obesity in Central America and the second-highest prevalence
of overweight, after Nicaragua. Although less severe than among women,
overnutrition among men, has resulted in rates of overweight averaging
around 48 percent throughout the isthmus and rates of obesity ranging
from near 5 percent in Honduras to more than 15 percent in neighboring
Guatemala. Obesity has increased rapidly in recent years, especially in
low-income groups who, as their income improves, buy foods with higher
fat/high carbohydrate content, often to the detriment of grains, fruits, and
vegetables. Progressive urbanization often includes an increased sedentary
lifestyle that compounds the deleterious health effects of a poor diet.

Common Health Consequences of Overweight and Obesity

The connection between excess weight and illness is well established
in nutrition studies. The risk for hypertension, atherosclerosis, cardio-
vascular disease, and high cholesterol is well documented and known

to accompany dietary transitions such as those taking place in Central America. As the diet becomes richer in saturated fat, people experience increased cholesterol rates and subsequent health effects. Among adults, this has included illnesses of circulatory systems such as ischemic heart disease (IHD). Common in the Western, industrial societies such as the United States, IHD is caused by a diminution in blood supply to a portion of the heart muscle that may result in necrosis or myocardial infarction. A narrowing of coronary blood vessels by atherosclerosis (a deposition of cholesterol on the walls of blood vessels) is now a significant cause of illness and death in Central America (Table 7.5).

The causal association of obesity with diabetes mellitus implicates it further. More than 85 percent of people who develop type 2 diabetes are considered overweight or obese, according to the Centers for Disease Control and Prevention. Diabetes occurs when the body loses its ability to produce insulin or develops a resistance to it. Hyperglycemia, or raised blood sugar, is a common effect of diabetes, which over time leads to serious damage to nerves and blood vessels. Diabetes has rapidly become a global epidemic. Approximately 6 percent of the adult population in Central America suffers form diabetes. The World Health Organization projects that diabetes deaths will increase by more than 50 percent worldwide in the next 10 years (Table 7.6).

TABLE 7.5
Selected Annual Disease-related Mortality Rates in Central America, 2002 (%)

	Belize	Costa Rica	El Salvador	Guatemala	Honduras	Nicaragua	Panamá
Ischemic heart disease (IHD)	10	16	13	3	11	10	12
Cerebro-vascular disease	8	7	4	3	7	7	11
Diabetes mellitus	4	3	3	2	5	5	6

Source: Data retrieved from Death and Daily estimates by cause, 2002, http://www.who.int/entity/health info/statistics/bodgbddeathdalyestimates.xls.

TABLE 7.6

Prevalence and Extrapolated Prediction of Diabetes Cases in Central America by Country

Year	Belize	Costa Rica	El Salvador	Guatemala	Honduras	Nicaragua	Panamá
2000	50,000	76,000	103,000	139,000	81,000	68,000	59,000
2030	150,000	237,000	320,000	447,000	269,000	246,000	155,000

Source: Data from Global Prevalence of Diabetes: Estimates for the Year 2000 and Projections for 2030. Wild S., G. Roglic, A. Green, et al. *Diabetes Care.* 7 (2004): 1047–53.

Programs for Nutritional Amelioration

Food and nutrition are keystone issues throughout Central America, as they relate intimately to poverty, urbanization, and various factors of the natural environment. In addition to departments and agencies within national ministries of health, education, or agriculture, a veritable alphabet soup of international and foreign agencies are involved in food programs. The FAO (Food and Agricultural Organization), UNICEF (United Nations Children's Fund), CARE, CRS (Catholic Relief Services), OxFam, (Oxford Committee for Famine Relief), Red Cross, USAID (United States Agency for International Development), and WFP (World Food Program) also of the United Nations all provide support to the region. Some programs are independent, operating on their own in specific countries. Other projects are linked up in regional level efforts. The following section includes illustrative examples including school meal programs and food fortification programs now operating in the Central American countries most affected by malnutrition.

The concerted interest in promoting good health and nutrition is not new in Central America. More than 100 years ago, the Pan American Sanitary Bureau originated after the Second International Conference of American States. Since its inception in 1902, the organization has been committed to improving the health of Latin American people. In 1949, the Pan American Sanitary Organization aligned with the World Health Organization (WHO) ,and the former began serving as the Regional Office of the WHO for the Americas. In 1958, the Pan American Sanitary Conference changed the name of the organization to the Pan American Health Organization (PAHO).[13] The broad commitment to combating disease, lengthening life expectancy, and promoting physical and mental health required PAHO to create several regional centers such as the Institute of Nutrition of Central America and Panamá (INCAP) to focus on delimited tasks and/or areas.

The Institute of Nutrition of Central America and Panamá (INCAP)

Inaugurated in Guatemala in September 1949, INCAP has grown rapidly in professional capacity to serve the applied nutrition needs of member countries. Over the decades, INCAP has become one of the most outstanding centers in the world for research, training, and development programs. Specialists work on projects targeting food analysis and food quality control, management of nutrition-related diseases, food-based socioeconomic studies, and food and nutrition education, particularly those promoting maternal and child health and nutrition. During the 1960s, for instance, INCAP provided technical support to the member states to conduct first national nutrition surveys that today constitute the baseline against which changes in the nutritional status at country and regional levels are measured. Throughout the ensuing decades, INCAP directed their efforts toward the development and dissemination of knowledge, technologies, and information that would ultimately improve the food and nutrition situation for people throughout the region.

Food Fortification

One of the most widely publicized INCAP programs began in 1955 as a research program for the development of a locally available food for use in weaning infants and feeding young children and other people suffering from PEM. The goal was to create a food with the approximate protein value of milk fortified with a complement of other nutrients. A low-cost, concentrated source of protein was available in the form of cottonseed flour, a by-product of commercial cotton production. This was combined with whole ground maize and other ingredients to yield a food similar taste and texture to *atole*, the traditional maize-based beverage consumed by a large population, especially in the highlands of Guatemala.

What came to be known as *Incaparina* was mass-produced in Central America in the 1960s and sold as a low-cost alternative to milk. To test its efficacy and safety, INCAP has conducted numerous studies including the INCAP Longitudinal Study of Growth and Development. This study has, among other achievements, helped establish the standard use of anthropometric indicators for evaluating the nutritional status of populations and determining the effectiveness of nutrition intervention programs.

From 1969–1977, children in four Guatemalan villages were randomly assigned to receive regular supplements of either fruit juice or an Incaparina beverage. Those in the Incaparina group showed improved growth rates and a reduced prevalence of stunting at age 3 years.[14] Incaparina has been the subject of both praise and criticism in numerous scientific papers published over the past 30 years. It is well known all over the world, primarily because it was a homegrown solution to undernutrition. Incaparina was also successful because its form was consistent with the dietary customs and taste preferences of the people. Finally, development experts laud the Incaparina program as an example of successful transfer of technology from intergovernmental agency to private industry.

Incaparina is now a commonplace beverage food of Guatemala and other Central American countries. In 1998, an improved formulation for Incaparina was developed. Another protein source replaced the cottonseed flour, and the new formula included revised micronutrient content based on the more recent scientific evidence. INCAP's current program includes strengthening efforts to improve technological-scientific capacity and the organization of training and research workshops for member countries. To date, INCAPs programs have yielded measurable gains in reducing rates of infant mortality, hunger, and poverty. INCAP was one of the first nutrition centers that contributed to knowledge on the interaction between PEM, infections, and vitamin A.

The process of fortifying foods has a long history in Central American food culture. As described in Chapter 3, the ancient practice of *nixtalmization* includes adding calcium to the flour to make it more palatable and, fortuitously, more nutritious. Currently, food is deliberately fortified by industrial mills, both to restore nutrients lost during food processing (known as enrichment) and to add nutrients that may not be present naturally in food and/or deficient in the diet. Fortifying common foods with vitamin A, iodine, and iron has proved one of the most sustainable and cost-effective strategies for delivering key micronutrients. One of the first programs was the iodization of salt. Studies carried out by INCAP in 1952 revealed that 38 percent of the Guatemalan population exhibited some degree of goiter. To improve the iodine status of the population, the government made mandatory the addition of iodine to salt. Goiter prevalence was reduced from 38 percent in 1952 to 5 percent in 1967.[15] Under the coordination of INCAP, iodized salt programs have been implemented in all Central American countries with high levels of success. Despite their pioneering role in the initiative, Guatemala's program has not been well conducted, and in the most recent assessment only 55 percent of households consume iodized salt. An increased prevalence of goiter has recurred.

When a 1965 survey showed that 26 percent of preschool-age children in Guatemala suffered vitamin A deficiency, INCAP responded by developing a sugar fortified with vitamin A. Sugar was the preferred vehicle for delivering the nutrient because most people consume it regularly, and it was the lowest cost food source of energy available. Following suit, Costa Rica, Guatemala, Honduras, but Panamá instituted regulations for addition of vitamin A to sugar in the 1974–1976 period. Vitamin A deficiency (VAD) has been significantly reduced in Guatemala, Honduras, and El Salvador through sugar fortification. Currently, Costa Rica has plans to reactivate its program, but Panamá has discontinued sugar fortification, as VAD is no longer a significant public heath concern.

Maize remains the dominant grain consumed in most of Central America, although wheat flour consumption has steadily increased. Several countries in the region began to fortify wheat flour with iron in the early 1960s. To address a whole range of nutrient deficiencies, including especially anemia, all the countries in the region agreed on uniform standards for fortification of wheat flour with iron, folic acid, thiamin, riboflavin, and niacin in 2002. Industrially milled maize flour has also been enriched with iron and some brands have included B_1, B_2, and niacin in some locations. Although some nutritionists criticize the practice of food fortification, arguing that the segment of the population with the greatest need for enhanced nutrients is typically unable to buy fortified foods, fortification of wheat flour in 1997 was implemented in Costa Rica and resulted in an effective public health impact. Rates of folic acid serum l deficiency detected in fertile women in 1996 decreased by 87 percent in urban areas and by 63 percent in rural areas.[16] The programs of salt and sugar fortification and interventions to prevent and control iodine and vitamin A deficiency are well established across the region; however, this has not yet happened with cereal flour fortification, and the full effect of this intervention is yet unknown. INCAP laboratories remain active in researching and evaluating these programs. Standards for the fortification of breakfast cereals, milk, and margarine are also being developed in some countries along with efforts to involve commercial manufacturers to provide more information on food composition and nutrient content.

FOOD AID PROGRAMS

A basic objective of national food policy is to provide food security, a situation that exists when all people at all times have physical, social, and economic access to sufficient, safe, and nutritious food that meets their dietary needs and food preferences for an active and healthy life.[17] The recurring and prevalent problems facing Central America, including those detailed previously, makes achieving *food security* difficult even in times of relative or localized prosperity. To some extent, all countries in Central America rely on programs of food allocation organized by domestic and foreign, private, and public agencies to aid in the attainment of food security. Food programs generally involve the distribution of rations or supplements of some form. One of the most important programs is the provision of food for school-age children. Children are a special risk for food security. Even short periods of malnutrition can permanently stunt the brain development of children, and malnourished children develop more slowly physically and underperform academically.

Food for Schools

In Guatemala, programs providing food to schools have been in operation since the 1980s. In urban centers, the Ministry of Education provides school breakfasts of fortified biscuits and Incaparina, to around 57,000 students annually. The WFP plays a direct role by distributing food to schools in food-insecure communities in the countryside and extra-urban areas, providing one meal a day during the 160-day school year. In Honduras, the Healthy Schools Program began in 1998 in rural and marginal urban areas to positively affect the people's living conditions that were displaced or otherwise affected by Hurricane Mitch. In the program, the WFP centralizes and distributes donated foodstuffs through schools to teachers and mothers who prepare the meals for the children. More than 300,000 students are provided a lunch during the school year and participate in school gardening projects to learn food production techniques and augment their daily food intake. El Salvador participates in the Healthy Schools Program as well, distributing rations to more than 650,000 students annually.[18] In Nicaragua, the school food program aims primarily to improve school performance and reduce dropout rates through a food program. Through its Ministry of Foreign Affairs' International Development Program, the government of Japan supports a project supplying milk to 200,000 children at 1,200 Nicaraguan schools. During the course of the project, school attendance rates of primary school students have increased by 10 percent and the rate of participation of parents in school events has risen by 20 percent. Other countries in the region have limited or targeted efforts in food programs.

Merienda escolar (school lunch), Honduras. AP Photo/Ginnette Riquelme.

Food and Nutrition Education Programs

Another approach toward food security involves education through community-level food and nutrition education programs. These programs contribute to improvements in the nutritional status of the poor by strengthening, modifying, or changing existing food habits. With support from the World Health Organization and Ministries of Health, INCAP developed the GUÍAS ALIMENTARÍAS or dietary guidelines in 1997. The guidelines, along with educational messages, aimed to improve the eating habits of the population in general to promote health and prevent nutritional disorders. As a visual aid in teaching activities, posters were developed with easily recognizable food ingredients. In Panamá and Costa Rica, posters contained the familiar food pyramid; however, an *olla* or kettle is used in the Guatemala campaign to illustrate basic food groups.

On the bottom tier, cereals and root crops occupy a full third of the area, conveying their importance as a base to the diet. Vegetables and fruits occupy the next level, and meats and dairy products share the much smaller penultimate level. Oils and sweets top off the charts with recommendations that they be used sparingly. The effort involved the distribution of some foods, but most rely on mass communication campaigns, training activities, and teaching materials to reorient the food and nutrition habits of the populace. Specifically, people are guided to:

- Eat a variety of commonly available foods.
- Eat sufficient grains, roots, vegetables, and fruits.
- Minimize the consumption of saturated fats, cholesterol, and oil.
- Minimize the consumption of sugar and sweets.
- Maintain a healthy weight.[19]
- Enjoy good food.

NOTES

1. *UNPD Human Development Report 2007/2008*, "Table 1: Human development index."

2. Ibid.

3. George M. Foster, *Hippocrates' Latin American Legacy. Humoral Medicine in the New World* (Langhorne, PA: Gordon and Breach, 1994).

4. M. E. Miller and K. Taube, *An Illustrated Dictionary of the Gods and Symbols of Ancient Mesoamerica and the Maya* (New York: Thames and Hudson, 1997).

5. Marianna Unow, *Maya Medicine* (Albuquerque: University of New Mexico Press, 2003).

6. FAO (Food and Agricultural Organization of the United Nations), *World Agriculture: Towards 2015/2030*, ed. J. Bruisma (London: Earthscan Publications).

7. FAO (Food and Agricultural Organization of the United Nations), *The State of Food Insecurity in the World, 2004. Monitoring Progress Towards the World Food Summit and Millennium Development Goals* (Rome: FAO, 2004).

8. E. Espindola, *Poverty, Hunger and Food Security in Central America and Panama* (Santiago, Chile: Naciones Unidas, CEPAL, Social Development Division, 2005).

9. FAO (Rome: FAO, 2004).

10. WHO (World Health Organization) Global Database on Anaemia, http://www.who.int/vmnis/anaemia/en, retrieved on May 12, 2008.

11. *Nutritional Evaluation of the Population of Central America and Panama. Regional Summary (1965–1967)*, Institute of Nutrition of Central America and Panama, and Nutrition Program, Center for Disease Control. U.S. Department of Health, Education and Welfare, Publication No. (HSM) 72-8120.

12. J. E. Casterline, L. H. Allen and M. T. Ruel, "Vitamin B-12 Deficiency Is very Prevalent in Lactating Guatemalan Women and Their Infants at Three Months Postpartum," *Journal of Nutrition* 127 (1997): 1966–72.

    13. H. R. Acuña, "The Pan American Health Organization: 75 Years of International Cooperation in Public Health," *Public Health Reports* no. 92 (1977): 537–44.

    14. Susan Jeffrey, "Childhood Nutrition Linked to Adult Intellectual Function," *Archives of Pediatric Adolescent Medicine* 162 (2008): 612–18.

    15. *A Short History and Current Situation of the Salt Iodization Program in Guatemala,* ed. Omar Dary, Ph.D. Food Fortification Advisor, MOST/The USAID Micronutrient Program (2004), http://www.mostproject.org/Updates_Feb05/salt.guatemala.pdf, retrieved on April 5, 2008.

    16. Luis Tascan Chen, and Melany Ascencio Rivera, "The Costa Rican Experience: Reduction of Neural Tube Defects following Food Fortification Programs," *Nutrition Reviews* 62 (2004): s40–s43.

    17. FAO (Food and Agricultural Organization of the United Nations), *The State of Food Insecurity in the World, 2001* (Rome: FAO, 2002).

    18. E. Espindola, *Poverty, Hunger and Food Security in Central America and Panama* (Santiago, Chile: Naciones Unidas, CEPAL, Social Development Division, 2005).

    19. *Food Based Dietary Guidelines and Health Promotion in Latin America. Pan American Health Organization. Food and Nutrition Program Division of Health Promotion and Protection.* Institute of Nutrition of Central America and Panama (INCAP) (April 1999) http://www.fao.org/ag/agn/nutrition/education_guidelines_pan_en.stm, retrieved June 3, 2008.

Glossary

aceite   Oil.

aceituna   Olive (*Olea europaea*).

achiote   Small, hard red seeds known as annatto; used as seasoning and food coloring (*Bixa orellana*).

adobo   Salt and spice mixture, dry or paste; used in preparation of meats.

aguacate   Avocado, fruit and leaves (*Persea Americana*).

ají   Capsicum, hot peppers (*Capsicum annuum*).

ajo   Garlic (*Allium sativum*).

alberja   Pea (*Pisum sativum*).

almendra   Almond (*Prunus dulcis*).

almuerzo   Early lunch or brunch.

amaranth   Leaves and seeds of annual flowering food plant (*Amaranthaceae* spp.).

amáraco   Marjoram (*Origanum* spp.).

ambulantes   Mobile marketer street food sales person carrying wares on foot or by cart.

anacardo   Cashew (*Anacardium occidentale*).

anafres   Small clay or metal brazier for cooking or warming foods over hot coals.

ananá　Pineapple (*Ananas comusus*).

annatto　See *achiote.*

antihito　Appetizer.

arepa　Thick, often filled, tortilla common in Panamá, Costa Rica; similar to *pupusa.*

arroz　Rice (*Oryza sativa*).

asado　Roast.

atole　Beverage prepared with cooked corn and other ingredients.

ayote　Gourd, pumpkin, summer squash (*Cucurbita pepo*); winter squash (*C. maxima*).

azafrán　Saffron (*C. sativus*).

balché　Leguminous tree (*Lonchocarpus violaceus*) and the Mayan fermented beverage made from it.

baleada　Thick, wheat flour tortilla folded in half and filled with mashed fried beans.

barbacoa　Barbeque.

batata (dulce)　Sweet potato (*Ipomoea batatas*).

batido　Milkshake.

berenjena, berengena　Eggplant, aubergine (*Solanum melongena*).

boniato　Sweet potato (*Ipomoea batatas*).

budare, budari　See **comal.**

cacahuete　Ground nut, peanut maní (*Arachis hypogea*).

cacao　Cocoa (*Theobroma cacao*).

cachito　Pigeon pea (*Cajanus cajan*).

calabacera　Calabash gourd (*Lagenaria siceraria*).

calabacín　Marrow, courgete (*Cucurbita pepo*).

calabacino　Dried, empty gourd.

calabaza　Pumpkin, squash (*Cucurbita pepo*).

caldero　Large, heavy-duty cooking pot.

camamila　Chamomile.

camote　See *boniato.*

caña　Sugarcane (*Saccharum*) or a liquor made from sugarcane.

canela　Cinnamon (*Cinnamomum zeylanicum*).

casabe　Cassava bread.

cassava Yuca, manioc (*Manihot esculenta*).

cazuela Clay cooking pot.

cebolla Onion (*Allium cepa*).

cena Supper.

ceviche Raw or lightly blanched fish-marinated in limejuice and chilies.

chacmole Maya sauce of **achiote,** chili, allspice, and tomato used often in game dishes.

Chapin Nickname for Guatemalans.

chaya Leafy vegetable, cooked and eaten like spinach or used as a wrapper (*Jatropha aconitifolia*).

chayote Pale to dark-green skinned small squash (*Sechium edule*).

chicha Fermented corn beverage, term also refers to beverages generally in some places.

chilan Small anchovy-like fish from Lake Atitlan, Guatemala.

chile Capsicum pepper (*Capsicum annuum, C. frutescens*). This term is generally applied to all species and varieties of hot pepper.

cilantro Leaves of coriander plant (*Coriandrum sativum*).

cocina Kitchen.

coco Coconut (*Cocos nucifera*).

cofradías Religious/social fraternal organizations that sponsor religious celebrations for patron saints.

comal Flat clay or iron grill.

comedor Dining room or informal restaurant serving typical food.

comida Main meal of the day; early dinner.

culantro a culinary and medicinal herb (*Eryngium foetidum*) known also as Bhandhanya, Chardon benit, Culantro, Donnia, and Culantro Coyote (also known as Fitweed or Long coriander).

curandera/curandero Traditional folk healer using herbal medicine.

curtido Spicy cabbage slaw served with **pupusas** and **vigorón.**

desayuno Breakfast.

elote Fresh maize, usually on the cob (*Zea mais*).

epazote Pungent green herb, used in cooking beans (*Chenopodium ambrosioides*).

ereba Garifuna term for **casabe.**

feria   Celebration or market day.

fogón   Stove or oven.

fonda   Small restaurant, **comedor,** also **soda** or **sodita** in Costa Rica.

fresa   Strawberry (*Fragaria* sp.).

frijól   Bean (*Phaseolus vulgaris*).

gandul   Pigeon pea (*Cajanus cajan*).

gifiti   Herbal infused rum; medicine used by Garifuna.

girasol   Sunflower (*Helianthus annuus*).

guaro   Distilled cane sugar alcohol; known also as *aguardiente*.

güirila   Stuffed tortilla made from young white maize.

guisado   Stew.

guisante   Pea plant, pea seed (*Pisum sativum*).

güisquilles   See **chayote.**

habichuela   String bean (*Phaseolus vulgaris*).

hierba buena   Spearmint (*Mentha* spp.).

higo   Fig (*Ficus carica*).

hoja santa   "Holy leaves"; used as wrappers for tamales or chopped into
stews. (*Piper sanctum*).

huerta   Vegetable garden.

izote   See **Yucca.**

jaca   Jackfruit (*Artocarpus integrifolia*).

jardín   Garden.

jengibre   Ginger (*Zingiber officinale*).

jícama   Yam bean (*Pachyrhizus erosus*).

jicara   Calabash gourd. Also dried fruit from the jicaro tree, or the decorative drinking container made from the same.

jitomate   Tomato (*Lycopersicon esculentum*).

leche   Milk.

lechuga   Lettuce (*Lactuca sativa*).

legumbre   Legume.

lenteja   Lentil (*Lens esculenta*).

licuado   Blended fruit and ice beverage.

limón   Lemon (*Citrus limón*).

Llanuras   Coastal plains with large expanse of level or rolling land, usually with few trees.

maíz   Maize, corn (*Zea mays*).

mamey   Soft, melon-like tree fruit (*Pouteria sapota*). See **sapote.**

mango   Mango (*Mangifera indica*).

manioc   Cassava or yucca (*Manihot esculenta*).

mano   Cylindrical stone muller or grinder used with **metate.**

manzana   Apple (*Malus domestica*).

manzanilla   Chamomile (*Matricaria chamomilla*).

marañon   Cashew (*Anacardium occidentale*).

masa   Dough made from ground nixtamalized maize used in making tortillas and tamales.

masa harina   Flour made from ground nixtamalized maize.

melón   Melon (*Cucumis melo*).

membrillo   Quince tree and fruit (*Cydonia oblonga*).

menta   Mint (*Menta* sp.).

metate   Grinding stone.

milpa   Garden plot where maize, beans, and squash are grown along with other plants.

miltomate   Husk tomato, **tomatillo** (*Physalis ixocarpa*).

mirasol   Sunflower (*Helianthus annuus*).

molcajete   Stone or ceramic mortar for grinding seeds or sauces.

mora   Blackberry, mulberry (*Rubus*).

nacatamal   Large, stuffed *tamal*, typical of Honduras and Nicaragua.

Nahuatl   Languages and dialects of the indigenous peoples of Central America and Mexico.

ñame   Yam (*Dioscorea* sp.).

naranja/naranjo   Orange (*Citrus aurantium*).

nixtamalization   Soaking process for removing the hulls or pericarps from tough skinned varieties of maize. The resulting pozole, or hominy, is used for making **masa.**

nopal   Prickly pear cactus (*Opuntia ficus indica*).

ofrenda   Altar constructed at home or in cemetery.

olla   Round unglazed clay pot.

orégano Several herbs are called orégano in Central America. Most commonly refers to Mexican Oregano (*Lippia berlandierei*).

Padrino Godfather or sponsor.

papa Potato (*Solanum tuberosum*).

papusa Thick maize tortilla stuffed with meat, beans, or vegetables and topped with **curtido.** The national dish of El Salvador.

pasa Raisin.

pepino Cucumber, gherkin (*Cucumis sativus*).

pepitas Pumpkin seeds.

pib Maya pit barbecue oven and foods prepared therein.

piloncillo Hard, brown sugar cones.

pimienta Black pepper (*Piper nigrum*).

pimiento (picante) Capsicum pepper (*Capsicum annnuum, C. fretescens*).

piña Pineapple (*Ananas comosus*).

pinole Toasted maize flour, dissolved in water to make beverage of same name.

pinolero Nickname for Nicaraguans.

plancha Large, flat metal cooking surface.

plátano Plantain; large thick-skinned cooking banana eaten as dessert when ripe, and as a vegetable when green (*Musa*).

pozole Hominy made from nixtamalized maize kernels.

puchero A meal of stewed meats: beef, sausage, bacon, and various vegetables or the pot in which it is cooked.

pupusa National dish of El Salvador; a thick, corn tortilla filled with meats, cheeses, refried beans, or pork rinds.

raspado Shaved ice and fruit syrup confection sold by street vendors; also known as *granzada* in Guatemala.

recado Savory mixture of annatto and herbs for use in Mayan **pib** cooking.

repollo Cabbage, col (*Brassica oleracea*).

romero Rosemary (*Rosmarinus officinalis*).

ruguma Long, woven basket used in detoxifying bitter **cassava** by Garifuna people.

sancocho Hearty soup or stew including chicken, fish, plantains, yuca, cilantro, yams, corn, and potatoes; typical of Panamá.

sapote Sapodilla fruit and tree (*Manilkara achras*).

seta Mushroom.

soda, sodita See **comedor.**

sofrito Aromatic mix of pureed of tomatoes, peppers, cilantro, onions, and garlic, herbs, and spices, used as a base flavoring and seasonings for numerous dishes.

sopa soup

tamal Nixtamalized maize dough wrapped in leaf and steamed.

tamarindo Tamarind (*Tamarindus indica*).

te Tea (*Camellia sinensis*).

tejolote Pestle for use with **molcajete.**

Ticos Nickname for Costa Ricans.

tomate Tomato (*Lycopersicon esculentum*).

tomatillo See **miltomate.**

tortilla Thin maize flour pancake, typical daily fare of Central America.

vigorón Nicaraguan dish of pickled cabbage, tomatoes, and onions with yuca and fried pork skins.

yuca Cassava (*Manihot esculenta*).

yucca izote Edible flowers and roots (*Yucca aloifolia* and Y. *guatemalensis*).

zanahoria Carrot (*Daucus carota*).

Resource Guide

GENERAL INFORMATION

Adams, Richard N. "Cultural Components of Central America." *American Anthropologist* 58 (1956): 881–907.

Bauer, Arnold J. *Goods, Power, History: Latin America's Material Culture*. Cambridge, UK: Cambridge University Press, 2001.

Bulmer-Thomas, V. *The Economy of Central America since 1920*. Cambridge, UK: Cambridge University Press, 1988.

Carrasco, David, ed. *The Oxford Encyclopedia of Mesoamerican Cultures: The Civilizations of Mexico and Central America*. New York: Oxford University Press, 2001.

Coe, Michael D. *The Maya*. 5th ed. New York: Thames and Hudson, 1993.

Coe, Sophie D. *America's First Cuisines*. Austin: University of Texas Press, 1994.

Coe, Sophie, and Michael Coe. *The True History of Chocolate*. London: Thames and Hudson, 1996.

Counihan, Carol M. *The Anthropology of Food and Body: Gender Meaning and Power*. New York: Routledge, 1999.

Crosby, Alfred W. Jr. *The Columbian Exchange*. Westport, CT: Greenwood Press, 1972, 2002.

Denevan, Wm. M., ed. *The Native Population of the Americas in 1492*. Madison: University of Wisconsin Press, 1976.

Flandrin, Jean-Louis and Massimo Montanari, eds. *Food: A Culinary History*. New York: Columbia University Press,1999.

Foster, George M. *Hippocrates' Latin American Legacy: Humoral Medicine in the New World*. Langhorne, PA: Gordon and Breach, 1994.

Foster, Nelson, and Linda S. Cordell, *Chiles to Chocolate*. Tucson: University of Arizona Press, 1992.

Fussell, Betty. *The Story of Corn*. New York: Alfred A. Knopf, 1992.

Goody, Jack. *Cooking, Cuisine and Class*. Cambridge: Cambridge University Press, 1982.

Gosden, Chris, and Jon Hather. *The Prehistory of Food: Appetites for Change*. New York: Routledge, 1999.

Harlan, Jack. *Crops and Man*. Madison, WI: American Society of Agronomy, 1992.

Lange, Frederick, ed. *Wealth and Hierarchy in the Intermediate Area*. Washington D.C.: Dumbarton Oaks, 1992.

MacLeod, J. Murdo. *Spanish Central America: A Socioeconomic History 1520–1720*. Berkeley: University of California Press, 1976.

Sanabria, Harry. *The Anthropology of Latin America and the Caribbean*. Upper Saddle River, NJ: Prentice Hall, 2007.

Super, John C. *Food, Conquest and Colonization in Sixteenth-Century Spanish America*. Albuquerque: University of New Mexico Press, 1988.

Super, John C. and Thomas Wright. *Food, Politics and Society in Latin America*. Lincoln: University of Nebraska Press, 1985.

Viola, Herman J. and Carolyn Margolis. *Seeds of Change*. Washington, D.C.: Smithsonian Institution Press, 1991.

Wesley Cowan, C. and Patty Jo Watson, eds. *The Origins of Agriculture: An International Perspective*. Washington, D.C.: Smithsonian Institution Press, 1992.

COOKBOOKS

Behnke, Alison, Griselda Aracely, and Chacon and Kristina Anderson. *Cooking the Central American Way: Culturally Authentic Foods, Including Low-Fat And Vegetarian Recipes*. Minneapolis, MN: Lerner Publications, 2005.

Cordova, Regina and Emma Carrasco. *Celebración. Recipes and Traditions Celebrating Latino Family Life*. New York: Doubleday, 1996.

Cox, Beverly, and Martin Jacobs. *Spirit of the Earth. Native Cooking from Latin America*. New York: Stewart, Tabori and Chang, 2001.

Fleetwood, Jenni, and Marina Filippelli. *The Food and Cooking of Caribbean, Central and South America*. London: Anness Publishing, 2004.

Majzlik, Linda. *A Vegan Taste of Central America*. London: Jon Carpenter Publishing, 2005.

Morton, Lyman. *Yucatan Cook Book: Recipes and Tales*. Santa Fe, NM: Red Crane Books, 1996.

Ortiz, Elisabeth Lambert. *The Book of Latin American Cooking*. New York: Alfred A. Knopf, 1979.

Saralegui, F. *Our Latin Table*. Boston: Little, Brown & Company, 2005.

White, Christine D. *Reconstructing Ancient Maya Diet*. Salt Lake City: University of Utah Press, 1999.

WEB SITES

Arecetas.com el Portal de Recetas del Mundo. Central America. http://www.arecetas.com/america/index.html.

Carnegie Library of Pittsburgh. "Latin American Food and Cooking." http://www.carnegielibrary.org/subject/food/latin.html.

Cocina del Mundo. "Cocina de Centroamerica." http://www.cocinadelmundo.com/continentes/central_america.html.

Global Gourmet. http://www.globalgourmet.com/destinations/.

INCAP—The Institute of Nutrition of Central America and Panama (in Spanish). http://www.sica.int/incap/.

Pan American Health organization (in English). http://www.paho.org.

World Institute for Conservation & Environment (WICE). http://www.natureworldwide.info/cam/central_america.htm.

Selected Bibliography

Acuña, H. R. "The Pan American Health Organization: 75 Years of International Cooperation in Public Health." *Public Health Reports* 92, no. 6 (1977): 537–44.

Adams, Richard E. W. "Archaeological Research at the Lowland Maya City of Rio Azul." *Latin American Antiquity* 1, no. 1 (1990): 23–41.

Bauer, Arnold J. *Goods, Power, History Latin America's Material Culture*. Cambridge, UK: Cambridge University Press, 2001.

Berdegué, Julio A., Fernando Balsevich, Luis Flores, and Thomas Reardon. "The Rise of Supermarkets in Central America: Implications for Private Standards for Quality and Safety of Fresh Fruits and Vegetables." http://www.rimisp.org/getdoc.php?docid=898.

Bressani, V., E. Benavides Acevedo, and M. A. Ortiz. "Changes in Selected Nutrient Content and in Protein Quality of Common and Quality Protein Maize during Tortilla Preparation." *Cereal Chemistry* 67, no. 6 (1990): 515–18.

Bromley, R. J., and Richard Symanski. "Marketplace Trade in Latin America." *Latin American Research Review* 9, no. 3 (1974): 3–38.

Bunzel, Ruth. *Chichcastenengo: A Guatemalan Village*. Locust Valley, NY: J. J. Augustin, 1952.

Coe, Sophie D. *America's First Cuisines*. Austin: University of Texas Press, 1994.

Crosby, Alfred. W. *The Columbian Exchange: Biological and Cultural Consequences of 1492*. 30th Anniversary Edition. Westport, CT: Greenwood Press, 2003.

Davidson, W., and Melanie Counce. "Mapping the Distribution of Indians in Central America." *Cultural Survival Quarterly* 13, no. 3 (1989): 37–40.

Denevan, William M. *The Native Population of the Americas in 1492*. Madison: University of Wisconsin Press, 1976.

Espindola, E. *Poverty, Hunger and Food Security in Central America and Panama*. Santiago, Chile: Naciones Unidas, CEPAL, Social Development Division, 2005.

FAO (Food and Agricultural Organization of the United Nations). *World Agriculture: Towards 2015/2030*. ed. J. Bruisma. London: Earthscan Publications, 2003.

FAO. *The State of Food Insecurity in the World, 2004. Monitoring Progress Towards the World Food Summit and Millennium Development Goals*. Rome: FAO, 2004.

FAO. *The State of Food Insecurity in the World 2001*. Rome: FAO, 2001.

Food Based Dietary Guidelines and Health Promotion in Latin America. Pan American Health Organization. Food and Nutrition Program, Division of Health Promotion and Protection, Institute of Nutrition of Central America and Panama (INCAP) April 1999, http://www.fao.org/ag/agn/nutrition/education_guidelines_pan_en.stm.

Foster, George M. *Hippocrates' Latin American Legacy. Humoral Medicine in the New World*. Langhorne, PA: Gordon and Breach, 1994.

Gonzalez, Nancie L. *Sojourners of the Caribbean: Ethnogenesis and Ethnohistory of the Garifuna*. Urbana: University of Illinois Press, 1988.

Helms, M. W. *Asang: Adaptations to Culture Contact in a Miskito Community*. Gainesville: University of Florida Press, 1972.

Herlihy, Peter H. "Central American Indian Peoples and Lands Today," in *Central America: A Natural and Cultural Area*, ed. Anthony G. Coates. New Haven: Yale University Press, 1997.

Institute of Nutrition of Central America and Panama, and Nutrition Program, Center for Disease Control. U.S. Department of Health, Education and Welfare, Publication No. (HSM) 72-8120.

Kirchhoff, Paul. "Mesoamérica." *Acta Americana* 1 (1943): 92–107.

Kufer, J., N. Grube, and M. Heinrich. "Cacao in Eastern Guatemala: A Sacred Tree with Ecological Significance." *Environment, Development and Sustainability* 8 (2006): 597–608.

Kunow, Marianna. *Maya Medicine*. Albuquerque: University of New Mexico Press, 2003.

Lentz, David L., Marilyn Beaudry-Corbett, Maria Luisa Reyna de Aguilar, and Lawrence Kaplan. "Foodstuffs, Forests, Fields, and Shelter: A Paleoethnobotanical Analysis of Vessel Contents from the Ceren Site, El Salvador." *Latin American Antiquity* 7, no. 3 (1996): 247–62.

Mangelsdorf, P. C. *Corn: Its Origin, Evolution and Improvement*. Cambridge, MA: Belknap Press, 1974.

McDonald, Michael R. "Learning Island Foodways, Tasting Ethnographic Methods" in *Anthropological Notebooks: Journal of the Slovenian Anthropological Society*. Contributions to Anthropology of Food and Eating 12, no. 1 (2006): 35–48.

Miller, Mary E., and Karl Taube. *An Illustrated Dictionary of the Gods and Symbols of Ancient Mesoamerica and the Maya*. New York: Thames and Hudson, 1997.

Monteith R. S., P. W. Stupp, and S. D. McCracken. *Reproductive, Maternal, and Child Health in Central America: Trends and Challenges Facing Women and Children*. El Salvador, Guatemala, Honduras, Nicaragua. Atlanta: Centers for Disease Control and Prevention, 2005.

Morton, J. *Fruits of Warm Climates*. Miami, FL: Julia F. Morton, 1987.

Nietschman, Bernard. "Hunting and Fishing Focus Among the Miskito Indians, Eastern Nicaragua." *Human Ecology* 1, no. 1 (1972): 41–67.

Nolan, Mary Lee. "The European Roots of Latin American Pilgrimage," in Crumrine & Morinis eds. *Pilgrimage in Latin America*, eds. N. Ross Crumine and Alan Morinis. Westport, CT: Greenwood Press, 1991.

Pagden, A. R., and J. Philip O'Hara (editors and translators). *The Maya: Diego de Landa's Account of the Affairs of the Yucatan*, Chicago, IL: J. Phillip O'Hara, 1975.

Pinto Soria, Julio César. *Raíces históricas del Estado en Centro América*. Guatemala City: Universitaria de Guatemala, 1980.

Prufer, Keith, and W. Jeffrey Hurst. "Chocolate in the Underworld Space of Death: Cacao seeds from an Early Classic Mortuary Cave." *Ethnohistory* 54 (2007): 273–94.

Recinos, Adrian. *Pedro De Alvarado, Conquistador De Mexico y Guatemala*. Panuco, Mexico, D. F.: Fondo De Cultura Economica, 1952.

Reina, R. E., and R. M. Hill. *The Traditional Pottery of Guatemala*. Austin: University of Texas Press, 1978.

Rogers, D. *The Domestication of Women*. London: Tavistock Publications, 1981.

Scaglion, Richard. "Kumara in the Ecuadorian Gulf of Guayaquil?" In *The Sweet Potato in Oceania: A Reappraisal*, eds. C. Ballard, P. Brown, R. M. Bourke, and T. Harwood, New South Wales: University of Sydney Press, 2005.

Schivelbusch, Wolfgang. *Tastes of Paradise A Social History of Spices, Stimulants, and Intoxicants*. New York: Vintage Books, 1992.

U.S. Department of Health, Education, and Welfare, and the Instituto de Nutricion de Centro America y Panamá, Guatemala City, Guatemala. "Nutritional evaluation of the population of Central America and Panamá. Regional Summary (1965–1967)." U.S. Department of Health, Education, and Welfare (DHEW) Publication no. (HSM) 72-8120. Washington, D.C., 1972.

Vila Rojas, Alfonso. "The Maya of Yucatán," in *Handbook of Middle American Indians*. Vol. 7, Ethnology, eds. Evon Z Vogt. Austin: University of Texas Press (1969): 24–75.

Wilk, Richard. Home Cooking in the Global Village, Caribbean Food from Buccaneers to Ecotourists. New York: Berg Publishers, 2006.

Wisdom Charles. *The Chorti Indians of Guatemala.* Chicago: University of Chicago Press, 1940.

Young, Phillip. *Ngawbe: Tradition and Change Among the Western Guaymí of Panama.* Illinois Studies in Anthropology 7. Urbana: University of Illinois Press, 1971.

Index

About the Author

MICHAEL R. MCDONALD is associate professor of anthropology at Florida Gulf Coast University.